MW00984280

WEASEL
WORDS

ALSO BY PAUL WASSERMAN

Information for Administrators. Cornell University Press. 1956.

Sources of Commodity Prices. Special Libraries Association. 1960.

The Librarian and the Machine. Gale Research Company. 1965.

Encyclopedia of Business Information Sources. Gale Research Company. 1971.

The New Librarianship. R.R. Bowker Company. 1972.

Consumer Sourcebook. Gale Research Company. 1974.

Speakers and Lecturers: How to Find Them. Gale Research Company. 1979.

Encyclopedia of Health Information Sources. Gale Research Company. 1987.

Encyclopedia of Legal Information Sources. Gale Research Company. 1988.

The Best of Times: A Personal and Occupational Odyssey. Omnigraphics. 2000.

New York from A to Z:
The Traveler's Look-Up Source for The Big Apple.
Capital. 2002.

ALSO BY PAUL WASSERMAN AND DON HAUSRATH

Washington, D.C. from A to Z:
The Look-Up Source for Everything to See & Do in the Nation's Capital.
Capital. 2003.

WEASEL WORDS

The Dictionary of American Doublespeak

PAUL WASSERMAN & DON HAUSRATH

A Capital Ideas Book

CAPITAL
BOOKS, INC.
Sterling, Virginia

Copyright © 2006 by Paul Wasserman and Don Hausrath

All rights reserved. No part of this book may be reproduced or utilized in any form or by any means, electronic or mechanical, including photocopying, recording, or by any information storage and retrieval system, without permission in writing from the publisher. Inquiries should be addressed to:

Capital Books, Inc.
P.O. Box 605
Herndon, Virginia 20172-0605

ISBN 1-933102-07-1   (alk.paper)

Library of Congress Cataloging-in-Publication Data

Wasserman, Paul.
  Weasel words : the dictionary of American doublespeak / Paul Wasserman and
    Don Hausrath.– 1st ed.
        p. cm. – (A capital ideas book)
  Includes index.
  ISBN 1-933102-07-1 (pbk. : acid-free paper)
  1. English language—United States—Jargon—Dictionaries. 2. Americanisms—
  Dictionaries. I. Hausrath, Don. II. Title. III. Series.

PE2839.W37 2006
427'.09–dc22

                                                                    2005019595

Printed in the United States of America on acid-free paper that meets the American National Standards Institute Z39-48 Standard.

First Edition

10 9 8 7 6 5 4 3 2 1

The authors dedicate this book
with love and gratitude
to our wives—

Krystyna Wasserman & Sydney Hausrath.

Contents

CONTENTS

Acknowledgments

We extend our very grateful thanks to the many friends and relatives who have made helpful suggestions about the content of this book, among whom Professor Richard Spear deserves special mention. Tim Hackman, librarian of the College of Information Studies at the University of Maryland, and Linda Christopherson of the College's administrative staff contributed in innumerable ways all through the preparation of the manuscript and members of Dr. Eileen Abel's 2004 class provided invaluable assistance with the research on a number of the book's entries. They included Jennifer Agresta, Shaileen Beyer, Chris Brady, Chris Eddie, Joan Goodhue, Elizabeth K. Howe, Keith Kisser, Trevor Rosen, Mary Catherine Santoro, Eva Tarnay and Jada Wells. John Howell provided a wonderful collection of language oddments, and we thank Sydney Hausrath for editing the manuscript.

Introduction

The closest I came to risking death for this book was trying to write notes from a National Public Radio interview while driving in downtown Tucson traffic. However, my co-author, Paul, would not have reached voting age had he not been pulled out of a frigid sea off the coast of France on December 24, 1944. Unlike almost 800 other American soldiers who lost their lives when their troopship, the SS Leopoldville, was sunk by a German submarine, he survived, learned to walk again in a Cherbourg hospital, and then reported back to his infantry unit in France.

You are likely thinking what does this have to do with this book on deception, of saying one thing and meaning another? Because that was my co-author's introduction to how easy it is to simply cover up a sad truth. The inept evacuation procedures employed in the SS Leopoldville disaster led to the greatest number of men lost in any troop transport sinking in the Second World War. It was kept secret by the US and British governments and the young survivors were warned not to write home about it. That is the sort of thing that would give you a jaundiced view of the workings of bureaucracies, be they military or civilian, even if we did not have many reinforcing lessons in years to come.

Our title includes the word doublespeak, meaning distortions and obfuscations and marketplace flim-flam. Doublespeak is not a term invented by George Orwell, but we surely nod to him for its origin, since he did invent "doublethink" and "newspeak" for his political novel, *1984*. Orwell, at 19 was abroad in Burma, posted in the delta region as a policeman in the British colonial service. Biographer Emma Larkin suggests his five years there as a government investigator colored his political outlook; certainly "five boring years within the sound of bugles" provided him a rich understanding of the workings of bureaucracies, organizations adept at word manipulation.

My own relationship to Orwell was based on my admiration for his book *Burmese Days,* so much so that when I entered the Army to attend what then was called the Army Language School, I requested Burmese from my smiling recruiting sergeant. I was, however, handed a stack of Russian textbooks in Monterey and was not to visit Burma until decades later when it had a military dictatorship with the Orwellian title of State Peace and Development Council.

Paul and I had collaborated on an earlier book, and we were used to exchanging notes on the daily inundation of news and information, but only as casual observers. Once in a while I would tear an editorial out of the New York Times and pin it up in my office for no good reason, or comment on the phone with Paul on a particularly outrageous, soul-grating term, so patently misleading you wanted to write it down and, like Miss Osgood's English assignments in Princeton High School, discuss. And so we did.

The book evolved as a sort of crib sheet, translating evasions, distortions, circumventions, obfuscations, and misleading terms back into English, a reader's and listener's companion to our 21st century. Both Paul and I have logged considerable time in various echelons of government and academic bureaucracies, which has provided excellent trolling for misused language. And we both lived abroad for long periods, where one naturally studies our American language from an alien perspective, which is helpful in learning our home country's use of indirection and evasions.

George Orwell developed a magnificent sensitivity for humbug, words that pretend to communicate but do not, and words at variance with the real meaning. Very likely, he would tell us our collection is no laughing matter, that we are being deceived and that if we accept these deceptions, our thinking and decision-making is flawed, controlled by the spin merchants of this world.

This list of words, then, is much like a collection of dusty carpets hung outside to air, with our definitions giving each term a good swat, allowing a clearer view at what is before us. For some of the terms, we simply try to bring clarity to that which is vague; others, we attack.

We invite you to join us in this language watch, and start your own notebook of questionable terms. There are, for example, understatements to avoid the truth, such as "economic adjustment" for recession. There are broad abstractions for an unacceptable term or idea: "downsizing" for slashing employment, masking words such as "preowned" for used, and PC euphemisms such as "economic deprivation" for being poor. Some terms, making a lie sound truthful, include the now classic Watergate use of "covert action" to replace burglary. There are conglomerating terms that shade the real state such as "midlife crisis" for the complex of middle-age needs. Many words we collected alleviate discomfort for the speaker, for example, "revenue enhancement" for taxes. There are terms that simply rotate the meaning to its opposite, such as "American Way" for special interest. There are obfuscating terms that pretend to communicate but do not, such as "in God we trust," and pompous escalation of a concept, such as "Oval Office" for President, and words that qualify on multiple grounds, such as "improper source dependence" for plagiarism. We included many of today's marketplace terms, such as the ubiquitous, "you may already be a winner," "some assembly required" or "your call is important to us." While not really deceptive, we could not resist sprinkling the text with some of the rich popular culture terms that are sprouting about us such as "dittohead," "dispose in an environmentally correct manner" or "do your own thing."

In preparing this book, we had, to use a military term, "a target rich environment." It is sad Orwell is not here to wonder at the inventiveness of "evidence free" testimony, on "weapons of mass destruction," "sound science" or "evil biology."

INTRODUCTION

Some of the world's most talented people are working, as this book goes to press, on ways to temper what is with what they want you and me to believe. George Kennan noted, "There is nothing in a man's plight that his vision, if he cared to cultivate it, could not alleviate. The challenge is to see what could be done, and then to have the heart and resolution to attempt it." This collection, hopefully, will polish your glasses, or better yet, improve your vision.

—DH

WEASEL
WORDS

Abdominal protector   Body armor used in boxing, cricket, baseball, hockey and other sports, protecting the male genitalia.

Above the line   Someone who makes a major contribution to movies or TV commercials, whether as director, writer, producer or performer, by dint of creativity and talent.

Above the rim   Reference to high jumping slam-dunking basketball players, thus an expression for the top, the best in hip hop.

Absorb   Besides the touted quality of a paper towel's ability to take up moisture, used geopolitically to dignify the taking of territory by force or less often, by treaty, commonly without involving the inhabitants in the selection of their new government overseers.

Academic dismissal   A polite way of saying a person has been kicked out of college.

Academic freedom   The liberty of the instructor to express opinions openly and without fear of reprisal by the employing institution or the state or the danger of losing a teaching job for expressing unpopular, heretical or politically controversial views. It further implies that at the university level particularly, no matter how unpopular the research that is conducted, academics will be protected in their jobs and are to be insulated by their institutions from outside non-academic pressures to pursue knowledge without restriction from law or public pressure.

Academic quality   That will o' the wisp that demands at every level of education the finest faculty, well-motivated students, a rigorous curriculum, consistent and meaningful grading methods, an administration composed of those who can enunciate a vision of the program to the faculty, the community, the student body, parents and prospective benefactors and standards that reflect consensus in what students should be held accountable for learning. This is all much easier said than done, but be it an elementary school or a university, you will find their brochures claiming that indeed, theirs is a program of the highest and most distinctive quality possible.

Academic rank   The term has multiple meanings such as a class ranking of a student's performance in a school, the comparative ranking of academic achievement of different schools, or, as it is most commonly employed, to characterize one's position or status in academia. In the higher education world the pecking order runs from professor, down through associate professor, then assistant professor, and finally, the lowly instructor, a sort of warrant-officer rank. Subtle adjectival distinctions abound: there are adjunct, visiting or research professors. When in doubt, the universally accepted salutation is doctor, signifying the holder has a doctoral, medical or ecclesiastical degree, or would like all others to believe that he or she does.

Academic tenure   This arrangement ostensibly exists to foster freedom of professional expression on any and every controversial question without fear of censorship or reprisal. In practice it frequently tends to shelter the out of date, the incompetent and the uninspired at the student's expense, with a guaranteed job for life.

Access charge   When you drop two quarters in a public telephone, pass money to a toll taker at a bridge or highway, or make use of a computer network, you have experienced this kind of payment.

Accident   Among its many meanings, the inability to control the muscles that control defecation or urination. Also, a not over-planned pregnancy. For more ominous failures, see nuclear accident.

Accordion scheduling   Companies that make use of part-time or temporary workers can cut overhead costs by never being over-staffed. They manage to do that by adjusting a worker's hours day-today, or, in some cases, telling someone working that "you can leave, we don't need you today after all." Of course, the accordion squeeze is on the hapless worker, not the company.

Acoustic privacy   To foster communication and interrelationships, office walls were ripped out from the 1980s onwards in favor of work pens, each inhabited by a person with a phone and a computer. The cubicle provided visual privacy—if seated—but interior designers overlooked the distracting noise of your neighbor's cell phone, speakerphone, smoker's cough and live conversations with fellow inmates. Retrofitting these cubicles with sound diminishing devices leads to the holy grail of the office space designer: visual and acoustic privacy. For the sake of the bean-counting administrators, designers ignore the obvious: to put you back in an office with four walls and a door.

Acting presidential   An undefined kind of graceful bearing and formal behavior expected of those representing the American people to the world. What is one person's acting presidential, however, is another person's aloofness. More often, the President or candidate is criticized for *not* acting presidential by falling down airplane steps, sexual dalliances, writing a profane letter to a music critic who criticized his daughter's singing voice, holding his dog by his ears, or more recently, running into your secret service escort on a ski slope and swearing at him. The Bush II term of office, however, demonstrates there is no requirement in acting presidential to conform to educated standards of grammar and pronunciation or to articulate a complex thought not previously crafted into sound-bite bullets.

Action   A multipurpose term that refers to first-hand involvement in a war, or what is sought after (wink, wink) in a city's hot spots, be it drugs, gambling, violence or sex.

Action news   Also known as eyewitness news. It typically takes place in a TV newsroom where the broadcasters stress realism by combining live accounts from newscasters at the scene with events captured earlier on tape.

Active consideration   A term meaning the application, manuscript or request has been stuffed in a file drawer, along with hundreds of others.

Activist judges   A negative term to mean a member of the judiciary who, it is claimed, "makes laws, doesn't interpret them." The term has appeared for a half century in Republican boilerplate, ever since Chief Justice Earl Warren's court ended school segregation with a unanimous ruling in the *Brown v. Board of Education* case in 1954. The term always applies to judges whose latest decision disagrees with a conservative's viewpoint. The phrase can imply (1) judges who attempt to resolve controversies, rather than passing them on to another court; (2) judges who strike down statutes or invalidate executive office actions; or (3) an incorrect exercise of the power of judicial review. Usually, this accusation is applied to a judge support-ing present day legislative guarantees of reproductive rights, affirma-tive action, claims of discrimination based on race, age, gender, and disability or worker and consumer protections. It does not seem to apply to the five conservative justices stopping the Florida recount, thus allowing the victory of Bush II. California Superior Court justice Richard Kramer—a Catholic and Republican—was painted with the "activist judge" label when he ruled that there didn't appear to be any "rational purpose" for denying marriage to gay couples. Previously, he had been lauded by conservatives for another ruling affecting marriage laws when an official of the Campaign for California Families observed, "Judge Kramer clearly recognizes the benefit of hearing all sides of the marriage debate, not just those arguments advanced by the same-sex couples and the Attorney General's office." *See also Strict construction.*

Activities stereotyping   At least one major publisher's guidelines for writers of publications for schools warns against stereotyping activities, such as showing men working with tools, older people fish-ing or women caring for children.

Actor   Political correctness requires we never add the sexist "ess" to this term.

Adhocracy   An organization characterized by an open-ended deci-sion-making culture which seeks to encourage staff members to work together across traditional arrangements to ensure the dynamism to achieve corporate goals.

Adjunct professor   This is the designation for instructors who offer classes in higher education programs, and whose only connection with the institution tends to be a contractual obligation to teach a course for far less compensation than is normally received by regular faculty members.

Administrative assistant   This company functionary was typically called a secretary in the past. In the light of contemporary sexual discrimination legislation and mores however, the role has been reclassified far more commonly than it has been transformed. In organizations with loftier pretensions, the person is referred to as an administrative professional.

Administrative leave   Being told not to come to work, usually due to an investigation of some sort. Police are placed on administrative leave after shooting someone, teachers after an alleged case of whacking a child.

Adventurist   Term applied to foreign governments that provide military, political or economic assistance to other nations when such support is perceived in Washington to fly in the face of American interests.

Advertorial   Advertising inserts replicating a publication's graphic style. To preserve the publication's credibility the insert usually displays the word advertisement and is printed in a slightly different typeface.

Advice   When the term is used by the police, your boss, or mother-in-law, as in "let me give you some advice," it is best to consider it an informal form of administrative decree.

Aesthetic imperative   Thanks to the modern day fixation upon appearance, style and gloss, female and male American consumers are opting for choices that transcend the merely functional, by seeking to express themselves by how they look, feel and are perceived. Virginia Postrel coined this term in her acutely observant book, *The Substance of Style: How the Rise of Aesthetic Value Is Remaking Commerce, Culture and Consciousness.*

Affected class   A sociological lens used to conglomerate groups vis-à-vis legislative proposals, legal matters, business and government practices. For example, the University of Washington requires an analysis be submitted with each proposed faculty hire assessing the labor pool considered for each affected class they consider: disabled veteran, Vietnam era vet, disabled, age 40 and above, Alaskan Indian/ Alaskan native, Asian/Pacific islander, black, and Hispanic. One can think of many more, including women, persons with disabilities, Asians, political refugees, economic refugees, or unemployed relatives of the department chair.

Afflicted   Several educational publishers' guidelines ban this term suggesting you use instead "a person who has (disease)."

After sales service provider   The title of the person with an 800- number to whom you are directed for problems you are having with an appliance or software and whose line is always busy.

After sales services   Better known as kickbacks.

Age-associated memory impairment (AAMI)   Brief forgetfulness, what all but health professionals call a senior moment.

Agents of virtue   Missionaries, development workers and "change agent" persons found in Africa and elsewhere who are well meaning but ill-trained and inept, thus producing as many problems as they attempt to solve.

Agit-prop   The phrase has its inspiration in the name for the Russian Ministry of Agitation that flourished in the mid 1920s. These days, the term is used to denigrate politically charged expressions found in the media, theater, art and music. It ranges from blatant propaganda to encrypted or symbolic messages, designed to appear nonpartisan while actually pushing a specific viewpoint.

Ain't no big thing   A polite hip hop response, usually to an apology.

Airline hijacking   Criminal commandeering of a single airplane for illicit purposes is clearly not the same as illegally seizing all the equipment and property of an entire airline company.

Almost certainly   In the "intelligence community," the term means there is a good chance the hypothesis is correct.

Alphabet method   The historic means of teaching reading by an emphasis upon learning letter names and spelling words aloud, usually in choral drill, until the letters of the alphabet, syllables and finally words are memorized, popularized by the famous McGuffey readers that America's schoolchildren learned with for three-quarters of the 19th century. Famed educator Horace Mann condemned the alphabet method, and encouraged the teaching of reading by presenting a limited number of words, for example, a picture of a dog with the word dog underneath.

Alternative language instruction   Educational jargon for teaching immigrant school children who have no knowledge of English in their own language.

Alternative music   Coined in the early 1980s to describe bands that didn't fit into the mainstream types of music of the time. It was an inclusive phrase for rock and similar forms and included post-punk, hardcore punk, hard-line punk, gothic rock, college rock and new wave bands. It remains to this day a supercilious characterization of every new form of musical expression that comes along having particular appeal to predominantly younger audiences.

America, love it or leave it   A slogan pasted on many a battered pickup truck that rejects any criticism of the US, its culture, its military position or any other aspect of the goodness of all things American.

American dream   This hackneyed phrase, much in favor in political parlance, can be defined however the listener chooses. In its broadest sense, it refers to the goals of enjoying a healthy family, a good home, a roomy car and a comfortable life style. In times of economic or military upheaval it shrinks for many to staying employed, keeping one's home, affording adequate health care and living a peaceful life.

American exceptionalism   A term almost as old as the country, likely an invention of Alexis de Tocqueville, but given new life by the Bush II Administration's view of America; a sort of ketchup bottle of goodness, spreading freedom and democracy on whatever barbeque it is squirted. If the meat gets burnt in the process, well, pardner, thet happens, ya' know.

American way   This is one more form of banal sloganeering that crops up time and again in politicians' rhetorical bluster and patriotic chest thumping. What it genuinely means is anyone's guess. Among its definitions: personal liberty, getting rich quickly, to mom, and picket fences and apple pie. In the Bush II Administration it translates into oversize tax cuts for the wealthiest, a burgeoning national deficit, the right to wage unilateral preemptive war and to temper regulatory restraints and to turning the controls of environmental pollution way down. The term has been incorporated into the name of a liberal advocacy group, People for the American Way, which supports a diverse democratic society and opposes those right wing groups who thought they had a head-lock on the term.

Amicable   Often followed by the word agreement, meaning both sides are mutually disgruntled by the outcome.

Analysis   The term, when used by a member of Congress, as in "my analysis of the situation," means the member has read and remembered the key points of the brief summary of the problem in a document put out by experts in the Congressional Research Service of the Library of Congress.

Anchor person   Don Hewitt, inventor of the term *Anchorman* in the pioneer days of TV news casting, has lived to see an educational text publisher suggest this non-sexist replacement.

Angry white males   Those bloc-voting, Caucasian, anti-minority, anti-feminist, anti-schools, ill-educated, mammoth-SUV-driving individuals with bumper stickers proclaiming, "Charlton Heston for President" or "I'm a hunter and I vote," unflagging in their support of President George W. Bush, considering him "a good guy," just like them. Presidential candidate John Kerry interrupted his intense campaigning in Iowa to tote a 12 gauge shotgun across a corn field reportedly in search of pheasants, but more likely, said the cynics, attempting to bag a few votes from this group.

Anniversary   Such as the 20th anniversary of the Gilroy Garlic Festival, a pretext for a celebration or PR spin.

Annual report   While presumably reporting the previous year's activities of publicly owned corporations to their stockholders, the text invariably conveys information well beyond the comprehension of the unwary reader because of the hyperbole of the prose and the obfuscated representation of the less appealing financial machinations of the company.

Anonymity   A term used by Internet users who seek to conceal their actual identities online. Besides the need to provide a unique moniker for your emails, various Web products are now offering remailing services that strip headers from messages, making it more difficult to trace a message back to its origin in an email, message board, or chat room. But court orders often force Internet Service Providers (ISPs) to reveal a subscriber's actual identity. These cases often involve critical postings about a company's products or services, and the company attempts to fight back against these anonymous accusations. The First Amendment protection of free speech has not provided a shield against such lawsuits.

Anti-flag, -family, -child and -jobs   Then House of Representatives minority whip, Newt Gingrich, included this phrase in his booklet, *Language, the Mechanism of Control,* that he mailed in 1990 to fellow Republican leaders across America. The booklet contained a list of "vivid, brilliant" positive words he suggested they use to characterize Republicans and negative words, such as these, to describe their Democrat opponents.

Anti-personnel weapon   The litany of military hardware that, simply stated, kills people, ranging from land mines and poison gas all the way to the neutron bomb. They all share the common objective of eliminating human life. Often, these specialized weapons can kill civilians or soldiers without excessive property damage, useful for city planners.

Anytime minute   While most explanations of connect rates for use of your cell phone are an example of industrial rococo, the one exception, as refreshingly simple as a Doric column, is this concept, whereby you can chat for a minute any time of the day or night for the same flat rate.

Appropriate   Used by bureaucrats to mask true levels of involvement, using the slippability of the term to mean what they want it to mean. For example, a May 13, 2004, Department of Defense background briefing on alleged violations of the Geneva Conventions for prisoner treatment discussed using "stress positions." A "senior military official" stated that such techniques used in prisoner interrogation must be "applied with appropriate oversight."

Approved alternative living arrangements   Commonly known at colleges and universities as off-campus housing.

Approved interrogation techniques   The declassified abridgement of the 2005 Vice Admiral Albert T. Church report on Department of Defense prisoner detention operations and interrogation techniques cited the deaths of two Afghan prisoners, stating that the abuse the two prisoners received "was unrelated to approved interrogation techniques," or more simply, they were beaten to death by personnel not following standard operating procedure (sop) torture methods. Those prisoners, who died during interrogation in 2002, were first certified by military officials as having died from natural causes but after scrutiny by the New York Times, Army investigators acknowledged the two were homicide victims.

Aspirational age marketing   A strategy employed by makers of consumer products enticing younger children to long for merchandise normally acquired by those older than twelve. Or, in the case of older adults, the strategy of showing products being swallowed, chewed or driven by persons at least a decade younger than the target audience. Exploiting tantalizing appeals to a kid's longings to feel older, advertisers offer pre-teens a wide array of clothes, cosmetics and electronic equipment. For the elderly, count on pill ads to show handsome middle-agers frolicking in Sunset Magazine settings.

Assault   In deference to the sensibilities of their audiences, this term is often employed by newspapers and broadcast media to characterize rape. Sometimes the term is prefixed by criminal, brutal or indecent.

Asset   When used in business this would normally connote items of value such as cash, inventories, capital equipment and the like. But in the world of international intrigue the term suggests spy or assassin.

Astroturfing   A term used to describe heavily orchestrated public relations campaigns paid for by corporations, but posing as grassroots movements, such as the "Citizens Right to Vote" ballot initiative in San Diego County, California. The Sacramento Bee reports that "a woman named Thelma contributed $100 to the campaign" and "the remaining $300,000 in contributions came from SDG&E," San Diego Gas & Electric, to fight San Marcos' plan to supply electricity at lower rates than SDG&E.

Asymmetric warfare   A 1970s social science term typically referencing the Vietnam War used by Department of Defense officials, including former undersecretary of defense policy Douglas J. Feith, who in 2004 identified such warfare as "a means for the weak to fight the strong." The phrase refers to those who are not part of a military force, but fall more into the category of saboteurs, partisans or terrorists attacking civilian or military targets, creating a form of guerilla warfare. The term connotes the uneven power structure of the belligerents: the one having an advantage in economic resources and firepower, the other greater endurance and flexibility. And just as George Washington and Ho Chi Minh were underdogs, they overcame the dominant power through use of allies and because the weight of the war on the greater power's domestic politics and economy became too great.

At liberty   Rather than enjoying a leisurely holiday, the term characterizes a person between engagements or out of a job.

At-risk children   A more sensitive term for what we used to call the children of the poor or slum kids.

At this point in time   Nixon Administration favorite for the shorter term, now. It subtly emphasizes, however, that one's vista might change with future events.

Atmospheric deposition of anthropogenic substances   Acid rain.

Atmospherics   A marketing term for the way a company appears based upon its offices, products, packaging and even the dress and deportment of its staff members.

Attention deficit disorder   To describe the many forms of contradictory and puzzling behavior characterized by developmentally inappropriate levels of attention, impulsiveness and hyperactivity. Children considered to have the disorder do not respond to cues from the behavior of others, are inept at taking turns, and have an impaired sense of time reflecting decreased ability to learn from previous experience, poor decision-making and risky behavior. Some reason that there is insufficient scientific evidence to support this label for unusual youngsters and that it is simply a way for parents and teachers to explain troublesome or unruly behavior. One of the consequences of the widespread diagnosis of the disorder: some 2.5 million children in American schools are being given Ritalin, an amphetamine, for this alleged disease.

Audible edibles   This is what people are heard consuming (popcorn being the favorite) while watching films and previews in a darkened movie theater.

Auditorily challenged   Those who suffer from hearing loss or deafness used to be called hard of hearing or simply deaf. No longer.

Authoress   Not PC like so many "ess" suffixes. If you want the playwright, who happens to be female, to appear on stage and not get pelted by neighbors' programs, shout "Author!"

Auto recycler   What used to be called a junkyard.

Automotive internist   If your bill looks a bit pricey, maybe it is because your car mechanic now uses this title.

Average   In education and government, the adjective implies barely adequate work or progress.

Average person   It is not PC to mention the "average man," according to any number of educational publishers' guidelines.

Aviator   A major educational publisher's guideline encourages use of this term by its writers, rather than the old-fashioned airman.

Axis of evil   These are the "regimes that sponsor terror," as defined by Bush II in his January 29, 2002, State of the Union Address. The phrase evolved from former Bush speechwriters David Frum and Michael Gargen, who were told to craft a rationale for dislodging the regime of Saddam Hussein. They wrote "axis of hatred"—with a nod to the "axis powers" of WW II—which the crusader syntax of the White House changed to the better-known phrase. The original idea was that the baddies were Iraq, Iran, and North Korea, with Syria added later.

B

B2B When businesses use the Internet to sell stuff to other business-es, in cyber talk.

Baby boomers The post-World War II generation of American men and women, often characterized by such traits as: work- and ambition-oriented, far more prone to divorce than their parents—as high as 50 percent—accepting of the authority structure, serious about life, optimistic about achieving success and far less skeptical and cynical about the world than the successor generation, Gen X. *See also Gen X.*

Backdoor draft The much touted Rumsfeld plan for a small, fast, high-tech military met its match in Iraq, where more occupation troops, heavier armored equipment, and more attention to garnering the support of locals were needed to control the mounting insurgency. Rumsfeld's miscalculation has meant the "reactivation" (sorry, you're not really discharged), mandatory enlistment extensions, while recycling National Guard troops back once more into the fray.

Background briefing The conduct of press conferences with media representations by government or military officials that are staged to present information about newsworthy military or political events as part of the effort to place on the public record details intended to portray such happenings in the most favorable light.

Backward country This is not politically correct, and is a term banned in many educational publications, with developing country used in its place. The World Bank uses the acronym LICUS (low-income countries under stress) and the British government refers to those at the bottom of the heap as "fragile."

Badly sourced   The term used by former Secretary of State Colin Powell to avoid saying false information, in reference to his reporting to the American people and the United Nations that the US possessed sure-fire "evidence" that Saddam Hussein was harboring weapons of mass destruction.

Bailout   When the federal government rescues a private company from bankruptcy by extending low interest loans or postponing tax payments—as in the case of the Chrysler Corporation. Also used to describe the way corporate titans sell their interests before the unknowing stockholders and staffers learn about the problems and lose their chance to do the same.

Bangalored   A term for a product or project, usually involving computer technology, such as reading of x-rays, processing tax returns or servicing computer customer desks, that has been moved to India, taking advantage of the low-paid highly skilled labor force available there via Internet and the fact they are working during the hours when most of the American labor force is home in bed.

Banner ad   That ubiquitous advertisement that appears on many a Web site. They have evolved into various standard sizes, which has facilitated a marketing bonanza for ad designers. These banners are developed by online advertising agencies and are instrumental in collecting new customers for a product or service, using direct response methods, and often are much more cost effective than using print media. A typical online advertising services company may contact a monthly customer base much larger than the total population of a major European country, those banners are responsible for companies offering ad-blocking services, methods of surfing with all graphics off, and variations to disable animations. These ads have resulted in a new phenomenon called banner blindness.

Banner blindness   A sort of Darwinian survival response by Web visitors to those ubiquitous banner ads, whereby the ads are tuned out of the consciousness. A 1998 study found that people often ignored banner ads, even when the ad offered information they were specifically looking for. Apparently people often skip over items that are different from the other items and particularly, to the distress of hot-shot page designers, large, colorful, animated items. Often, respondents could not even recall seeing the intrusive advertisements.

Barely used products   In a period when many devoutly hold to the conviction that the latest gadget will transform their life, more and more people are divesting "like new" electronic products. Often the product is simply too complicated for the prospective consumer. For whatever the reason, the Internet has become a national flea market for thousands of items labeled "new in box."

Barrista   The coffee served by someone using this title is likely to be more flavorful than that served at your local hash house, but it will also cost you twice as much.

Baseless   A derisive term used to dismiss questions from the press believed difficult to verify.

Bathroom tissue   Polite discourse for that essential—toilet paper.

Bay of Tonkin episode   The imaginative invention of an incident on August 4, 1964, by Lyndon Johnson claiming the North Vietnamese had attacked an American military vessel. That fabrication led Congress to authorize dramatically increased expenditures to step up the hostilities into a full scale—and still regretted—war in Vietnam.

Behavior transition corridors   Middle school educator talk for hallways.

Below-investment-grade securities   The designation by analysts of types of financial choices that include investing in common or preferred stock or corporate bonds (commonly termed junk bonds) of companies judged to be unstable or highly risky. These securities may prove highly insecure, and therefore potentially hazardous, to the financial health of those making such investments.

Beltway   A circumferential roadway that encompasses the nation's capital, within which resides the Congress, the federal bureaucracy and the local population. *Inside the beltway* suggests the nefarious doings within the branches of government, while *outside the beltway* refers to the citizenry innocently removed from the intrigues and compromises attributed to "beltway insiders."

Benign neglect   This theory held, albeit reluctantly, that for the benefit of the economically downtrodden, the very best remedy for their
unquestioned needs was simply to let them help themselves. The
concept was first professed by Daniel Patrick Moynihan when he
proposed it to the Nixon Administration.

Berkeley-quality software   A term likely invented by Stanford grads,
often abbreviated to BQS, meant to denigrate sloppy, inferior software, the concept being that the writer was possibly under the influence of drugs during its composition, that documentation is missing
or poorly done, or that the material has not been debugged.

Beta testing   A concept whereby select individuals are allowed to
test new or revised software programs before release to the public at
large. This allows a few nerds to try using the program and provide
feedback, but telling the rest of us, snake in the tree-like, no fruit for
you, kiddo. When a complex but "not released" upgrade is allowed to
be downloaded by thousands of users, is the company really interested in our test results? Is the product still in beta format? Maybe,
possibly, the marketing division was peering down from the branches
when the 2004 introduction of Google's Gmail or Microsoft's Service
Pack II was introduced.

Between jobs   Still another way to optimistically obfuscate the reality of being unemployed.

Big Government   Traditional conservatives such as Ronald Reagan
used the term as a pejorative, promising in his first inaugural address
to "curtail the size and influence of the federal establishment."
Corporations applauded this view, picked on as they were by regulatory agencies curtailing their smog emissions and other pollution
rights and even being told what they could claim in cigarette ads.
But the era of Bush II dismisses those views, albeit going along with
the rights of corporations to pollute. Bush's b.g. credentials include
creating a vast new prescription drug entitlement, proposing a $1.5
billion federal program to promote marriage and promoting a billion buck-a-day weapons-of-mass-destruction scavenger hunt
(switched shell-game-like to a "fostering democracy" effort) in Iraq.
No tax-and-spend Democrat, of course, as Democrats are character-

ized by their reliance on federal involvement in social issues, Bush II can be called a don't–tax–but–spend–and–allow–the–deficit–to–sink–the–economy Republican.

Biological parent   What used to be called one's mother or father, but now, with adoptions and the high percentage of children raised in homes with step-mothers or fathers, it has become a legal term to identify the persons who transferred a particular set of genetic characteristics to their offspring.

Biometric measures   The means of clearly authenticating the identity of an individual. Once it was simply collecting your fingerprint, but no longer. In this age of trust-not-thy-neighbor, a new generation of security measures is approaching: scanning retinas and irises, facial features and voice patterns. But for the foreseeable future, the chances are very good that the tried and tested fingerprint method will continue to be the most reliable automated biometric measuring instrument.

Biosolids   If you are a member of the Water Treatment Federation, an association representing the interests of sewage treatment plants across America, this is what you call sewage sludge.

Biosurgery   Flat on your back on a hospital bed is bad enough, without learning that this term means that you are likely allergic to antibiotics and thus will soon be seeing a healthcare professional place live maggots on your wound to clean out infected areas.

Bipartisan   Putting a happy face on the behavior of the other party when enough of its members yield to the opposition, thus allowing passage of legislation that cries out for reasoned debate and argument.

Birthing center   This is a place you can go to have a baby. It is staffed with midwives and nurses and typically is located outside a hospital. But often the center is close to a hospital in case of complications. Usually the mother and newborn child return home within hours of the birth. An attractive feature of birthing centers is that they cost less than a hospital stay.

Black Friday   Subsuming allusion to the financial panic of September 24, 1869, the term now refers to the day following Thanksgiving each year when retail merchants hopefully anticipate that the consumer tide will lift the shopping season into the black—profitability.

Bleeding heart   Connoting the tender sensitivities of those whose political sentiments would use the power of government expenditures to alleviate the distress of the needy.

Bling or Bling Bling   The term for the prevailing longing to look good and own (or at least lease) good stuff. Manifestations include Rodeo Drive jewelry and clothes, sports cars with names ending in i, wines from the store's locked case and soaking at sunset in one's private pool at a tropical resort eight time zones from your home. In sum, exhibiting an overpowering need to experience the finest the world of materialism has to offer.

Blogo ad   The term for a commercially sponsored blog, promoting a product. Blogo derives from blog and logo, since the corporate identity is usually included, albeit near the bottom of the page. The informality and personal views that make up your typical blog make for a different kind of marketing tool when gonzo companies such as Nike and General Motors start using this medium.

Blogs   Contraction of Web log or Weblog. These are personal sites that are frequently updated about "what's happening" with a person or a person's relationship to the Web. It is often a mix of personal journal and Web guide, but there are millions out there and each is a bit different, from an illustrated scrapbook of *My Trip to Disneyland*—so boring they are called Haircut blogs—to other personal experiences, interests, thoughts and views, family history, election preferences and God knows what. The blog is a tool for building like-minded communities on a vast array of interests, including, increasingly, political views. Automated publishing systems have simplified the process of blogging. While bloggers were once a manifestation of dedicated Web surfers, blogs are becoming accepted by those in the shallows of surfing, with blog sites being offered by the University of Minnesota library and big city papers such as the San Jose Mercury News and the Minneapolis Star Tribune. *See also Grassroots blogs.*

Blondenfreude   The guilty pleasure of finding enjoyment in learning the details of the misfortunes of such light-haired female corporate celebrities as Martha Stewart or Carly Fiorina.

Blood in the water   Since blood in seawater attracts sharks, the term refers to an event or activity that is bound to attract the attention of the media, government investigators or popular attention.

Blow-away   The usually accidental removal of computer files and directories.

Blow-back   Unintended and unanticipated consequences of an action, often of a political or economic nature. An example is what happened after US-supported forces in Afghanistan finished shooting at the Soviets—they turned their guns in the supplier's direction.

Blown away   Used in cyberspeak to mean a product whose market is destroyed by a new innovation, and in teen talk to mean a particularly devastating reaction.

Blue dog Democrat   A term denoting a coalition of about three dozen conservative to moderate Democrats, mostly from the South, who push for a balanced federal budget. The term is spin-off of a yellow-dog Democrat—a party loyalist who would vote for a yellow-dog on the ticket before crossing party lines—and provided a delightful symbol in the terrier-like blue dogs of Louisiana painter, George Rodrigue.

Blue ribbon panel   Sometimes called blue ribbon commissions. However it is disguised, such an entity has a preset time span and includes recognizable figures who are supported with funds and staff to carry out the mission. These panel members, experts, real or otherwise, often spend enormous amounts of (usually taxpayer-provided) money investigating a problem, sometimes real, but often political shadows projected on the walls of Plato's cave. The charge to these panels is to expose miscreants, or address changes in functions, procedures or organizational structure. Investigation topics include some of America's central problems; a tanking economy, suffering schools, or who's-on-first foreign policy issues. Congress and the White House, among others, favor such panels, often after considerable media prodding. The major limitation of panels is that by the time they issue their final report, their recommendations fall unheeded into the sea; the investigators' zeal has faded, the media has moved on to another issue and thus the report is filed and forgotten and the threatened organization reverts to its usual ways of doing business. In short, a blue ribbon panel is designed to do nothing but to do it splendidly.

Blue State *see* **Red State**

Boat people   Those who leave their home countries by boat and risk their lives on the open seas to escape their homelands' political oppression or economic blight. First used to characterize fleeing Vietnamese following Saigon's fall in 1975, but later the term came to encompass those seeking to emigrate from Haiti, Cuba and China.

Bobos   Characterizes those who populate the contemporary suburbs and exurbs who converge in personality, behavior and preference, seemingly antithetical aspects of bohemian cultures. The term was coined and elaborated in David Brooks' 2000 book, *Bobos in Paradise*.

Body bags   Large zippered cadaver pouches, usually of vinyl, used to convey a corpse to a burial site. Besides transporting those who died as the result of an accident or crime, those killed in US military operations are usually packed in such devices. A common euphemism for combat is "where the body bags are filled;" 56,000 were filled in Vietnam, and to date over 1,900 in Iraq, along with tens of thousands of Iraqis. *See also Dover Factor*

Body shopping   The practice of hiring people to work in an organization as temporary staff, thus denying them all the perks that go to regular workers.

Bonding   Besides the chemical process of fixing something to something else, it now means the act of sharing or friendship.

Book of Life   The popular term for the completion of the 3 billion part DNA sequencing that makes up the code of life in the human body. The achievement was announced by the White House in 2000, when interests from the Celera Corporation and the publicly financed Human Genome Project agreed they had achieved the goal simultaneously.

Boosting   Organized shoplifting by a trained and well-equipped team.

Bork   To bork is to attack a political figure or nominee for government appointment through negative characterizations in newspaper or broadcast media accounts. The reference is drawn from the controversial and unsuccessful nomination of Robert Bork to the US Supreme Court in 1987.

Bottom feeder   Just as some fish find their sustenance in the muck at the depths, this phrase echoes this concept by Springerizing human relationships on television, proclaiming Elvis lives at the grocery checkout stand and providing plotless films devoted to chases, splattered blood and a requisite humping—unrelated to the plot—that takes 120 minutes to get from A to B.

Brand bait   The way in which celebrated entertainment personalities are compensated for using a company's product in public situations where the firm's brand is sure to be seen. This is also called "roach bait."

Break a leg   It is difficult to imagine a more bizarre way of wishing someone good luck than by the use of this term, favored in the entertainment industry.

Breeder document   The primary document allowing one to obtain legitimate identification—such as a driver's license—for establishing a false identify. Often, the original document used to establish a false identify is a consular identification card (CID), which some governments issue to their citizens living in a foreign country. By using a variant of the spelling of a person's name, for example, a CID can create a new identity, which is helpful if you have entered the United States illegally.

Brought to you by   While one winces at the florid prefaces of 17th and 18th century writers addressed to their sponsors, we placidly accept this phrase followed by an advertising plug. Both are needed for the same reason: coin of the realm.

Brown cloud   Smog.

Brownfields   These are landfills, strip mines, garbage dumps and lightly polluted former industrial sites. Green parks and open spaces are to be found surrounding most wealthy neighborhoods, but poorer communities often have been living cheek by jowl with polluted, abandoned industrial parks. The 2002 Brownfields Revitalization and Environmental Restoration Act provides matching funds to revitalize some of the 750,000 brownfield sites across the nation, with the goal of turning them into "Greenfields," open spaces for public parks and recreation facilities as well as residential and commercial spaces. Conversion of brownfields provides an opportunity to provide needed recreation open space in inner cities. But the benefits of conversion of brownfields are not for the inner city poor alone—many of the nation's golf courses are built on former brownfields. *See also Greenfields*

Buckeye bunnies   Groupies who follow the Marlboro men of the rodeo circuit, gripping their dusty denims with a transient, albeit iron-fisted ferocity; displayed as well by the silver-buckled rustics atop a bucking bull.

Bummer   Today's sympathetic response to hearing bad news, what long ago would have elicited, "I'm very sorry to hear that."

Bundlers   A classic practice in political fundraising designed to give a collection from many donors more clout by combining efforts. Those who carry out the bundling role are the major campaign fundraisers of both parties, drawn from the ranks of corporate executives, lobbyists and financial titans, who fork out the maximum legally permissible sum of $2,000 and impress countless numbers of their friends, family members, business associates and employees to do the same.

Bunny hugger   A term whose meaning runs from someone concerned with the fate of wild species at one end to a militant animal rights activist on the other.

Burger King moms   The characterization for those mothers at the other end of the socioeconomic scale from soccer moms. This demographic profile would include those at the lowest rung of the economic ladder with the slimmest level of voter participation and election turnout, often single parents who are focused on paying bills, keeping kids adequately housed, fed and clothed. This sector includes a high percentage of immigrants.

Burn rate Just as you observe millions of dollars of rocket fuel blast a missile skyward at a space launch, investors watch their venture capital be consumed by entrepreneurs launching new companies. Thus, this term refers to "negative cash flow," funds used for project development, and often reported to venture capitalists in monthly installments, possibly to cushion the shock of the amount spent. The hope is that eventually the investment will generate a "positive cash flow," and investors can chuckle about their fears regarding ever getting an equitable return on their venture capital.

Cabinet   There is nothing in the US Constitution specifying that the President is to be served by a cabinet composed of the secretaries of the federal departments and other selected advisors. It has simply come into being as an expedient means of keeping track of Presidential rivals while conducting the business of the Executive Branch.

Cafeteria Catholics   Those who identify with the Church but reserve for themselves the prerogative of accepting and following only those tenets of the faith or the pronouncements of the Pope with which they are in agreement, such as abortion, gay rights or divorce.

Calculated risk   A term causing shudders to run up and down your spine, often spoken by politicians or one's military superior, implying a choice of action where the dangers are well beyond estimation.

Call me sometime   A dismissive, understood by both parties to mean the opposite of what is said.

Camouflage candidates   Another derogatory term coined by the wordsmiths of the National Rifle Association. These are Democratic candidates whom the NRA intends to expose: those who straddle the fence on gun control, i.e., who are accentuating their intention of allowing gun owners to keep their weapons, but stressing all the while the need for gun safety, a strategy the NRA derides as "posturing."

Camp   Artfully exaggerated affectation in style, quality or taste judged by the cognoscenti to be vulgar, venal or outrageous, or all three. In hip hop it can refer to prison or one's present location.

Campaign consultant Someone who offers services in advising, managing, financing or simply helping candidates during election seasons. Virtually anyone uses this appellation who has ever been paid for (or even volunteered) as an election door-knocker or envelope stuffer.

Capital punishment as deterrent Countless people believe the death penalty deters criminal behavior. But research studies looking at murder counts before and after the elimination of the death penalty reveal no evidence that execution is, in fact, a viable deterrent.

Captive auditors The language describing the sports fans in the stands subjected to vile shrieking of other spectators, who no longer emit cheers as frequently as obscene invectives shouted at the athletes and referees.

Carb-avoids To characterize those who are part of the growing hordes who reduce or simply eliminate from their diet those foods that contain carbohydrates, like breads, pasta and desserts.

Career alternative enhancement program What corporate personnel prevaricators suggested was the status of several thousand auto workers whose jobs were eliminated.

Career associate scanning professional What we used to call a grocery store checkout clerk.

Career change opportunity Similar to being offered a swimming opportunity from the plank of a pirate ship, you are about to leave your job involuntarily.

Career changes You are "between jobs," certainly better than that naked term unemployed. Better yet, you can be in "a transitional phase in career readjustment."

Carnivore A system allowing the FBI to eavesdrop on your emails without your knowledge or authorization. Carnivore is suspected of having the capability of not only reading your incoming and outgoing emails, but monitoring your Web-surfing and downloading habits, newsgroup posts and file transfers. The FBI claims they performed only eight Internet wiretaps in fiscal 2003, none using the multi-million dollar software they first named Carnivore and later renamed DCS-1000. In 2005, the FBI reportedly abandoned this custom-built software for eavesdropping on computer traffic.

Carry trade   The behavior of investors who take advantage during periods when interest rates are at a very low level to borrow money cheaply in order to invest in all types of markets.

Cash-flow   This is Bush II Administration's jargon for having to borrow beyond its April 2004 increase of the $25 billion "reserve fund" to bridge the funding gaps for its military operations in 2004. Since there was not enough money to actually pay for the Administration's operations in Iraq and Afghanistan and since 2004 was an election year—with the Pentagon saying they didn't need additional funds that year—the result was furtive borrowing. According to John Spratt, Jr., ranking Democratic member of the House Budget committee, this unadmitted shortfall results in "the deferment of maintenance, training or other important programs" and of course, less for its so-called war on terrorism.

Casting couch   The site in the offices of Hollywood titans where starlets seeking career-advancing roles granted horizontal favors to those they believed were in a position to reward them.

Census reductions   A convoluted way of stating a company is firing employees.

Chalk and talk   Educator's derisive term for a traditionally taught course, not one that is taught online or makes use of the Internet.

Chalkboard   What used to be a slate blackboard in a classroom until some enlightened individual started using much more visible green boards.

Challenge   These days, if Tonto were advising the Lone Ranger about being surrounded by attacking Apaches, it is doubtful he would have said, "You've got a problem, Kimosabe." Rather, keeping in the spirit of the times, he would have used the present day replacement for the p-word: "challenge."

Challenged   Replacing the word handicapped, this has become the presumably softer and more politically correct description for less-than-perfect individuals. Typically prefixed by a clarifying word such as "auditorily" challenged for those with hearing disorders or "educationally" challenged for those with a learning disability.

Character issue   In the political lexicon and reflecting the presumably higher moral standards of those who level the charges, this is the way to suggest that an office holder or candidate for office engages in extra-marital or promiscuously sexual behavior or, in a notable *Saturday Night Live* skit accusing Bruce Babbitt, then a presidential candidate, of "his long history" of exceeding the 10-item count in supermarket express lines.

Chargeback   This is the process for reversing charges on a credit card. You hand the ridiculous lamp your husband bought back to the merchant and request that the funds are returned to your account. Or you phone your credit card company and request that a fraudulent or disputed charge be reversed. Then, the credit card company hits up the retailer to return the funds to them. This is also a term for matrix organizations' transfer of funds from one department to another, "paying for" goods or services from another sector of the organization.

Chattering classes   A term dating from the 1980s when it was coined in Britain to connote the talking style and the content of those from loftier social and economic levels who espouse cosmopolitan values, attitudes and spending patterns and are thought to convey urbanity about erudite and arty subjects as well as public issues. More recently the phrase has come to include members of the media, particularly columnists, talk show hosts and pundits of all types.

Chick lit   A genre thought of in times past as the female literary tradition, but these days featuring books written by women and designed to appeal to them as well, centered in the quirky and often comical antics of a younger (20s to 30s) female heroine who leads an often confused love life and displays whimsical taste in clothing and other consumer products.

Chicken hawk   There are many in media punditry and political life who vociferously proclaim their martial bellicosity, but who avoided putting themselves at risk in the nation's military service. On the long roster of bunting-wrapped observers can be found Pat Buchanan, Rush Limbaugh, Tom Delay and Richard Cheney.

Chief Justice of the Supreme Court   While there is a Chief Justice of the US there is no such officer as Chief Justice of the Supreme Court. The individual who serves as Chief Justice is but one of the nine court members and is appointed like the other eight by the President with the advice and consent of the Senate. He is not elected by his peers and has but one vote, exactly like the other justices.

Chilean sea bass   Actually, *Dissostichus eleginoides*, family *Nototheniidae*, is not a member of the sea bass family. Pulled from the briny deep, it is distinguished by its ominous, shark-like maw—thus the name you never find on restaurant menus, the Patagonia Toothfish.

Choice   The term favored by those who prefer it to the harsher word—abortion. It implies a woman's right to choose whether she wishes to give birth to the child she is carrying or not. Contemporary culture tends to place the highest value on having a myriad of individual judgments, from choice of lifestyles to choice of identities to choice of telephone plans. All are seen to be inherent to the exercise of personal freedom.

Chokepoint   The term that has all but replaced bottleneck.

Cholo-Style   The appellation for the Mexican-American gangster style attire that began in the streets of East Los Angeles and is sweeping across the nation. It incorporates such elements of the tough guy look as oversize t-shirts, baseball caps, low-slung cargo pants and head bandanas and attracts female as well as male adherents among the young and hip.

Chronologically challenged   Since speaking of someone as old, aged or elderly became taboo, this is the way the more sensitive refer to those living out their final years.

Chutzpah   Derived from Yiddish, this conveys any or all of the following traits: unmitigated gall, righteous arrogance, supreme personal confidence, a supercilious sense of superiority, or unbridled self interest.

Civil commitment   The term for keeping a sex offender locked up after he or she has completed a sentence, but is judged to have a mental state predisposed to sexual violence and thus likely, if released, to commit another crime. State legislatures and prosecutors are employing this tactic to address the issue of women's substance abuse during pregnancy. To safeguard against "crack babies," where the fetus is injured by drugs during the pregnancy, the State of Minnesota, for example, can lock up women suspected of illegally using drugs for the duration of the pregnancy. *See also Preventive detention.*

Civil rights   In the 1960s this term was virtually synonymous with the cause of racial equality between blacks and whites—in schools, public places, the courts, employment, accommodations and services. Today, the issues revolve around discrimination against Arabs and Muslims, gays and lesbians and integration and legal and social justice for all other minorities as well as the defeat of bigotry in every context. Civil rights questions arise also in the more questionable violations of Constitutional rights and civil liberties of immigrants and foreigners stemming from the sweeping federal terrorism law provisions embodied in the USA Patriot Act.

Civil unions   Continuing same sex relationships that grant many but not all of the legal rights of marriage to the partners, after supporting legislation is promulgated by a state. The high tide of the anti-civil union backlash in many parts of the country has occasioned what has been called Civil Wars over the divisiveness of such legislation.

Civilian irregular defense soldier   Pentagon term for a mercenary.

Clarify   What is done in political or military speech after making a serious gaff in public expression. The corrective is to offer vociferous explanation, revision or restatement to correct any misunderstanding of what it was that the speaker ostensibly intended to utter. In effect, eating one's own words.

Class warfare   Political invective contending that the other party is actively seeking a rupture between the poor and working class and the wealthy. The instrument seen as widening the gulf is the fostering of legislation unfair or indifferent to the concerns of those who have less and need more from government.

Classified information   Those government files made inaccessible to those who wish to see them for personal or investigatory reasons. The restriction of access is claimed to support national security interests.

Clean bomb   Military jargon for a neutron bomb, one whose radiation effectively kills all men, women and children in a target area, but sends less radioactive material into the atmosphere.

Clean up the historical record   The procedure followed by politicians and despots in editing or changing the original records of activities or events by offering alternative versions to make them more acceptable to the public.

Clear skies initiative   George W. Bush's controversial decision to rewrite the Clean Air Act which, he announced in his 2003 State of the Union Address, would spare power companies the cost of investing in pollution controls when they upgrade their plants and thus increase emissions. Bush II claimed the old rules impeded economic growth and modernization, thereby reducing job levels. The initiative would have done nothing to reduce emission of carbon dioxide, which, of course, contributes to global warming, and would have delayed the enforcement of public health standards for soot and smog until 2015, while restricting the power of states to combat windblown pollution coming from their neighbors. The New York Times, in a May 7, 2004, legislative obit, writes, "Clear skies is a bad bill, which in the name of streamlining current law would offer considerably more relief to the industries that pollute the air than to the citizens who breathe it." The bill failed to make it out of a Senate committee in 2005, and stalled again on the Administration's second attempt.

Click-fraud   Everyone knows that your tour bus driver who stops at the "best" leather market gets a payment from the proprietor for bringing shoppers into the store. But suppose the proprietor is charged for a busload of imaginary tourists? It was bound to happen, with advertisers on Web sites being paid a fee for every time a potential customer is lured through an electronic door of an online market. Unlike the few bucks your tour bus driver receives for his efforts, for an ad that gets potential customers to click on it to find out, say, about legal advice, Internet gambling or travel offerings, the proprietor shells out well over a quarter a click. Thus, workers in India are paid $25 to $50 a week to be tap-tap-tapping at selected sites, running up the count. But those professional clickers' days may be numbered. Software programs can do the same fraudulent work for less. Further, fraud-detecting software is coming as well. Stay tuned.

Click-through   The process of responding to a Web ad by clicking on it to the advertiser's page. The counting of those responses, or click-throughs, provides marketers with a rough guide to the effectiveness of the online advertisement, much like counting customers who visit your store. This is known as your CTR or click-through rate. Of course, just counting visits to a site does not always correlate to a larger base of customers or users, since an ad that simply arouses curiosity may not have the bottom-line results of a site that is targeted to the needs of a specific group. Marketers take the cost of the advertisement and divide it by the number of click-throughs to come up with the CPC (cost-per-click) rate.

Climate leaders   Another initiative by George W. Bush that seeks to recruit the nation's industrial polluters to voluntarily find ways to reduce their pollutants by 10 percent or more within a decade. But only a tiny percentage of the thousands of companies that contribute to the troublesome rise of greenhouse gas emissions, which affect global warming have signed on. Most of the major utility companies prefer to participate in an industry-conceived plan called Power Partners, which does not commit companies to achieve specific goals.

Coalition forces in Iraq   This is the term the Bush Administration uses, whilst Arab broadcasters prefer the term "occupation forces."

Coconut   Derisive hip hop reference to a white-acting Hispanic person.

Code master   Designation for a physician working in a hospital emergency room who is successful in reviving those patients whose hearts have stopped beating.

Coded messages   Racially charged symbolism, like the measures to defend the preservation of the Confederate flag atop the South Carolina statehouse, that is a blatant political strategy to appeal to racist voters.

Coin-operated employees   A neologism for contracted employees who have replaced company staff for cost-saving reasons.

Collateral damage   Used extensively in military briefings to admit that the ground or air attack has inadvertently wrought destruction upon civilians or our military personnel who had the misfortune to be in the wrong place.

Collectible   If your aunt stores piles of old newspapers and cottage cheese cartons in her living room, the relatives will worry, but if she haunts eBay towards developing a definitive collection of A&P vegetable cans or photos of stop signs, she is simply into collectibles. A *very* collectible item, however, as explained by the mavens of *Antiques Road Show*, are items that several others are willing to pay hard cash for as well. Trinkets, oddments and curios are not always very collectible, and in fact, may fall into the category rudely termed "shelf shit."

Collective punishment   A legal term used in international law and the 1949 Geneva Conventions for the outlawed practice of destroying civilian property as a reprisal or deterrent. In violation of the Geneva Conventions, collective punishment in Iraq was reported in 2003 when US military forces bulldozed date palms, orange and lemon trees in Central Iraq to penalize farmers who did not provide information about insurgents attacking US troops.

Combat emplacement evacuator   It must have taxed the ingenuity of the Defense Department to come up with this alternative for the word shovel.

Comfort station   Public toilet.

Commercial broadcasting   The practice in which the US government extends freely to private profit-making companies the exclusive use of public air space to market their audiences to advertisers, without requiring from them any but the most negligible public service announcements.

Commitment   A political phrase favored by politicians bracketed by "my" and "commitment to ... revitalize (or) ... sustain, (or) ... lead our march on. ..." Regrettably, political followers seldom believe that after the election, their cause will continue to be of interest to the politician. Too often, the re-elected politician explains these same positions are not completely realistic, and they must bend to the give and take of political reality.

Common good   As in "it's for your own good," as mother ladled castor oil down your throat, the term has different connotations if you are the drinker or ladler. In the age of anti-government, religiosity, market ideology and self-interest, it is increasingly difficult to claim that building a dam in your district will provide cheaper electricity and diminish flood damage trumps the loss of still another lovely mountain canyon, or that lower gas prices are worth agreeing to the building of a refinery nearby. Those choices become political wedge issues with powerful interest groups asking, "What's in it for me?" Doing anything, especially something with a grandness of vision, is harder than ever, since as adults we have the right to participate in the decision-making and we have varying views on the efficacy of the proposed dose of castor oil. Likely the most valuable definers of common good are collectives such as the Food and Drug Administration or credentialing agencies such as the American Medical Association, a group of experts who make the decisions we have effectively delegated.

Community mobility   Neighborhood transportation plan for sharing vehicles of all types as a means of protecting the environment and reducing pollution.

Community setting stereotyping   A major school publisher's guidelines warns against providing illustrations of Asian Americans in a neighborhood composed solely of other Asian Americans, or African Americans living in an urban setting.

Company culture   The set of values, beliefs, myths and rites which characterize the identity and style of companies and govern the behavior of their managers and employees.

Companion animals   Pets, but not tapeworms, fleas, ticks, chiggers, giardia or similar creatures that might be accompanying you.

Compassionate conservative   Sloganeering rhetoric of right wing politicians to convey their heartfelt sympathies for those less fortunate, who, they profoundly believe, are best served when they help themselves through self-reliance and a stronger work ethic. George W. Bush, for example, has clearly demonstrated his campaign promise to be a compassionate conservative by constantly displaying his compassion for conservatives.

Competitive bidding   The policy of extending an open opportunity to submit a bid on the performance of a program or service for a government agency or company to all who wish to compete in order to win a contract for the work to be done by the lowest bidder. But it seldom plays out as simply as it sounds. Disgruntled losing competitors argue that cost and value are never the same thing and that an auction sets the goal at the lowest common denominator level without taking into account the value of unique skills or valuable past experience or relationships. Then there are the restrictions often introduced, such as giving preference to smaller businesses and minority- or women-owned firms. Perhaps the most celebrated recent skewing of the competitive bidding process took place in Iraq where only American firms were eligible to compete for the US military's business, resulting in huge contract awards to Halliburton and Bechtel.

Competitive equality   *See* **Corporate Welfare**

Comprehension   A term used by educators to mean the student can read. Usually this is then broken down by grade level, e.g., a fourth-grade level.

Computer literacy   Used for mastery of basic skills in the use of computers and the Internet as a modern day societal ability. The phrase originated with Andrew Molnar when he was directing the Office of Computing Activities at the National Science Foundation in 1972 to cover all the programs comprehended under his department. Today computer literacy is commonly deemed by specialists and educators to be as essential as the three Rs were in the past.

Conceivably   In spy talk the term means that there is little chance the hypothesis that follows is correct. Also bureaucratic weasel word meaning that the following comment has been included by an insistent member of the innumerable people who routinely "clear" a memo, but seems wacko to everyone else.

Conceptualize What we used to term thinking about something.

Confederacy of the mind Term coined by the American Civil Liberties Union to characterize those clinging to the tenets of the historic South reflected in their passionate support for and flaunting of the Confederate Flag.

Confidential memorandum With a wink and a nod, what is technically a message intended solely for internal communication is often leaked to an outsider as fast as a fax transmits. Such a document is invaluable for settling scores, criticizing, obfuscating, discrediting or claiming credit once it mysteriously finds its way into the clutches of a favored media outlet.

Confrontainment Television or radio performers on talk shows who revel in insults, obscenity or other forms of aggressive behavior generally directed at the participants or interviewees.

Connect the dots To develop a thesis from various pieces of evidence.

Conservation The host of concerns that engage the efforts of individuals, organizations and government agencies to protect against all manner of dangers seen as basic to safeguarding the health of the citizens and the quality of their lives as well as the resources of the nation and of the planet at present and in the years to come. Among the universal issues are the use of energy, the protection of the environment including fish, wildlife, waterways, forests, the atmosphere, the food supply, historic structures and more.

Consolidating Instead of forthrightly describing the shut-down or closing of factories and retail stores, public relations-attuned companies resort to this characterization, which they deem more pleasing to the ear of the public.

Consultation The pro-forma discussion with subordinates on an issue about which the administrator has already made a unilateral decision.

Contract with America In 1994 the Republicans used the promises contained in their "Contract with America" to conclude the 40-year Democratic control of the House of Representatives. Newt Gingrich was the architect of the contract and one of its most devout precepts was the absolute necessity of the federal government to live within its means by balancing the budget. When Speaker Gingrich and his followers swept into office in January 1995 they assaulted the Clinton Administration to bring fiscal responsibility to the nation's spending so that the US, just like America's families, would live without incurring a deficit. By the time Clinton left office in January 2001, the large budget deficit inherited from the first Bush Presidency had been replaced by a $236 billion surplus. Now in the fifth year of the Bush II Presidency the nation is again drowning in red ink, with the deficit hitting more than $300 billion in 2005. Newt is long gone but many of the Republican Congressmen who rode into office with him in the 1994 election are still in office. And one decade later the Republican-controlled Congress and White House preside over the largest deficit in American history with no relief in sight. The only conclusion to be drawn is that the "Contract with America" was a short one.

Controlled communication   The strategy of placing a leak proof zip-lock bag around information and facts about your administration or government agency that might be viewed by the public as reflecting negatively on your policies, programs or performance. The practice, both in using a zip-lock bag in your refrigerator, or the bureaucratic equivalent, is for protection. The public is assured that secrecy is necessary to safeguard national security and to maintain executive privilege.

Controlled economy   The description used for the means by which a non-capitalist state superintends the production, work and earnings of industry, commercial activity and labor by decisions made by the central authority and administered through its bureaucratic apparatus. Invariably this brings about inefficiencies and poor living conditions and sets severe limits on the fostering of a middle class.

Controversial   Classification used to typify political positions—as well as those who hold them—when such views oppose those of government authorities. Extremist is another term used to characterize what comic Roger Price called "wrong-thinkers and troublemakers." *See also Extremist*

Convalescent home   An institution, not a home, where people are usually not expected to get better, but to regretfully follow life's catabolic trend lines until death. Similarly, there are rest homes and nursing homes.

Converging forces   Military term meaning at some unspecified time in the future there will be, hopefully, a meeting of various troops; also a social science term for several abstract concepts considered together.

Core competencies   The concept that supports the idea that business and government do only what they do best and most profitably or efficiently and should pay someone else to do the rest. That is the rationale for the Pentagon decision to concentrate on fighting wars and to contract with private corporations for support. Thus, a new breed of camp followers: corporations such as Halliburton and its subsidiary Kellogg, Brown and Root to service the military's needs, including laundry, road maintenance and communications.

Corporate earnings   One might assume that this signified a company's official profits. But while this construct, for what are generally accepted accounting principles, is thought to be precise, it is often fraught with guesswork. The numbers, shown for reserves against possible losses on what a company is owed or projections of the exact expense level for closing a factory, are only two illustrations of where management numbers can be wide of the mark. Moreover, recent history has demonstrated how earnings are manipulated and investors repeatedly deceived because some companies simply cheat.

Corporate governance   Evidence in court cases and elsewhere demonstrates that the wishes of many shareholders have received short shrift from Corporate America's boards of directors. Board elections seldom bear any resemblance to democratic processes. The operating style is for stockholders to receive a slate of candidates nominated by the board, who then win their seats, whether or not most investors vote for them. Due to the number of recent corporate scandals that have aroused and dissatisfied stockholders, the

Securities and Exchange Commission has been trying to screw a latch on the accountability barn door by enacting new rules and significant changes in the regulations. Thus, after decades of non-representation, stockholders in publicly traded companies are beginning to have some hope for a more substantial role in the companies' decision-making.

Corporate reform   The movement that has gained enthusiastic public support to put in place safeguards to protect shareholders from derelict behavior and performance by managers and board members of public companies. The objectives were to ensure that no corporate official would be beyond the checks and balances of shareholders, corporate directors or the law. Among prescriptive remedial measures were: treating stock options as expenses in financial statements, ensuring the independence of boards of directors from management control, separating the auditing and consulting functions of public accounting firms, rotating the companies which conduct the financial auditing of public companies every few years and eliminating management conflicts of interest. Not surprisingly, once the earlier public indignation and media furor subsided, very little has been enacted that might fundamentally alter the age-old ways in which business is conducted in Corporate America.

Corporate welfare   This is the heaping pile of tax advantages and subsidies that certain businesses and industries receive through government largesse, including the armaments and aerospace companies as well as agriculture and the pharmaceutical industry. Their politically powerful constituencies, benefiting as they do from this bounty, prefer a more benign term, such as corporate tax-base lowering or competitive equality.

Cosmetologist   A person who used to work at what used to be called a beauty parlor.

Cost containment measures   Bureaucrat speak for cutting spending.

Cost-per-click   *see* **Click-through**

Cost shifting   The term for when Congress, addressing a popularly perceived national concern, passes a bill, but steps out of the room just before the waiter brings the bill, leaving 50 state legislatures to each dig out their wallets. The bipartisan National Conference of State Legislatures stated in 2004 that the Bush II Administration and the Republican-controlled Congress have socked it to the states to the tune of over $29 billion in "unfunded mandates" in the current fiscal year, with the next year's burden climbing to $34 billion. The organization pointed to two such programs, "No Child Left Behind" and "Individuals with Disabilities Education Act," as creating a shortfall for the states of almost $20 billion in 2004. Reacting to the Bush II Administration's fiscal year 2006 budget, Governor Mark Warner of Virginia and Arkansas Governor Mike Huckabee warned House and Senate leaders that the Bush II Administration can't simply shift Medicaid costs to states to cut the massive federal deficits and finance such Bush II priorities as Social Security reform.

CPC *see* **Click-through**

Covert operation Made famous by President Nixon's Watergate memo-writers to describe burglarizing the offices of the psychiatrist of Daniel Ellsberg, of Pentagon Papers fame.

Cramming This sophisticated form of fraud, also known as larding, is when telephone callers respond to ads, for example, telephone dating or adult chat links. Later they are unknowingly charged on their monthly phone bills for services they neither requested nor used. It works because many telephone-related services are paid through local telephone companies passing on the payments to the service providers. Criminals use a company that consolidates billing for service providers, allowing them to bill through the local companies and collect their fees by labeling the services with innocent-sounding titles that are hidden in the bills and thus go unnoticed by consumers.

Create a space Besides its use in interior design, it can also be used to mean a personal method of dealing with the world, as in Jerry Garcia's friend who always wore ice skates around his neck for that purpose, or in a spiritual sense, where an internal calm is triggered by such devices as yoga, meditation or music.

Creative accounting   The widespread practice in American corporations of issuing false, distorted or misleading reports of their financial
transactions.

Credibility gap   The reluctance of many political figures to own up
to unpalatable truths by denying or obfuscating the actual state of
affairs. When the lapse is construed to be a serious credibility gap
the public is less willing to accept the statement. Many recent Presidents have suffered from this malady: Lyndon Johnson's light at the
end of the Vietnam tunnel; Richard Nixon's, "I am not a crook;" Bill
Clinton's, "I did not have sex with that woman;" and George W. Bush's
will o' the wisp sightings of weapons of mass destruction.

Creep   A verb meaning to move slowly, a noun meaning an unpleas-
antly strange person, and lately, to have a sexual encounter.

Crew-member   A major school publisher's guidelines warn against
referring to *able-bodied seaman,* using this term instead.

Crime in the streets   A catch-all euphemism for the perceived threat
to life and property of the white suburban dweller from the black
inner city population.

Cross-pollinate   No longer just a term learned in Biology 101, it is
used now to describe the exchange of ideas and concepts between
various individuals. While the botanical concept results in the fertilization of a plant to allow it to bear fruit, the weekend workshop use
of the term often bears cockamamie ideas that fade quickly after the
euphoria of the "sharing" has worn off.

Crowd management team   Police units trained and deployed in
the nation's capital, and at other sites across the country, to ensure
that public protests and those who participate in them comport
themselves peacefully without endangering public or private buildings, institutions and businesses. Their tactics have ranged from simply cordoning off specific areas and maintaining a visible presence
to keep the protesters in check, to resorting to more aggressive and
forceful non-lethal means to bring demonstrators into line through
beatings, pepper spraying, stun guns, tear gas and rubber bullets or
arresting large numbers of protesters.

CTR   *see* **Click-through**

C

Cultural elite   A reference to that undefined group of individuals in academia, the entertainment world, the media and think tanks credited with setting the tone in society and influencing the national agenda and moral values by their pronouncements. The fantasy that this group conspires satanically to sway public opinion was spawned by the pronouncements of former Vice President Dan Quayle.

Cultural issues   The phrase spokespersons for police departments now use when speaking of bloodshed, beatings and riots caused by racial prejudice.

Cultural wars   The ongoing battles over social, political and economic issues, from abortion to gay marriage, fought by conservatives and liberals, be it on Capitol Hill, Internet sites, or talk radio.

Culture   Normally this term relates to matters like manners and good taste but in contemporary usage culture is reflected in the eye of the beholder and can employ whatever meaning the viewer perceives. In social science terminology cultural deprivation implies poverty. For Chairman Mao's Great Leap Forward and Proletarian Cultural Revolution, it meant the slaughter and persecution of entrenched bureaucrats, landowners, business people and followers of traditional social conventions.

Culture of life   Language of George W. Bush to describe the legislation he supported which makes illegal the type of abortion known medically as "intact dilation and extraction," used to terminate pregnancies in the second and third trimester of pregnancy.

Culture of poverty   The condition described by the right wing as those who are poor because they lack the moral strength and motivation to work harder to improve their deplorable existence.

Cup holder cuisine   Convenience refreshments that are packaged in containers to fit into a car's drink holder.

Currency adjustment   What a government tells its citizens when their money drops in value against the world's currencies. It is not the practice of governments, however, to explain to their citizens that the currency dropped because of failed policies of the government, be it a totalitarian regime whose policies failed, or an elected government whose citizens believed outrageous claims as to how, if elected, the politicians would lower their taxes, increase jobs, build needed infrastructure, provide for their well-being and improve their overall economy at the same time.

Customer   It seems that terms like patrons, clients and users have fallen into disuse. Instead, organizations as divergent as public libraries and the Internal Revenue Service see their public as market targets who thus become customers.

Customer relationship management (CRM)   Companies are using a variety of data analyses and modeling techniques to discover previously unknown patterns and relationships—called data mining. Information is collected from the Web as well as from other sources. Using various modeling techniques, companies can offer new products that they have good reason to believe meet specific customers' needs and interests. For example, a group that markets outdoor gear might learn that a sizable number of mountain climbers are also into rafting. Thus, their next offer might include rafting items in their catalog. CRM allows companies to predict which customers are likely to leave and provide them with a special offer. Data is provided to CRM companies from many sources, including credit card applications. If you have ever bought an item by telephone, caller ID combined with demographic data tells them still more about you. Whether you know it or not, merchants are collecting data on you and your preferences in very sophisticated associative databases.

CYA   For "cover your ass," the motivation for many a Washington, DC, self-serving memorandum, or innocently pointing a possible investigative finger in any direction but the writer's.

Cyberspace activist   A person leading the fight against governmental and corporate attempts to delimit Internet users' freedoms and rights. A cornucopia of issues confronts those individuals: copyright and intellectual property, free speech, civil liberties, encryption technology as well as disagreements related to political beliefs and cultural norms.

Cyclic looking   Washington, DC's new addition to the Mall, the National Museum of the American Indian, is not addressing in its displays the scientific evidence that Native Americans emigrated to America during the Ice Age, since Native American mythology has it that they were always here in the Americas. A curator explains, they look at things "very cyclically, not in a linear way."

Cynical   A term usually coupled with exploitation, be it of religion, the marketplace, or the law. It is a time-tested method to denigrate an opponent's position.

Czar   A recent inside-the-beltway term applied to the fall guy who must take charge of planning for a national problem overlapping several cabinet jurisdictions, such as drugs or energy, without the mandated authority or Congressional appropriations necessary to attempt a real solution.

Daddy Mac   Real estate verbiage for a mortgage assumed by parents to acquire homes for their children who are unable to assume the burden of paying off such a debt. Sometimes the property is in joint ownership.

Dark biology   *Hot Zone* author, Robert Preston, coined this term, which refers to scientific research associated with biological warfare.

Data mining   This is the term for sifting through data with a computer to identify patterns and establish associations and relationships. It is used in mathematics, cybernetics, genetics and other fields where you are looking for patterns—where one event is connected with another, or a sequence, where one event leads to another, or clustering, where you visually spot data anomalies, and forecasting, where today's data might indicate tomorrow's trends. This powerful tool is being used by federal security agencies and obviously could threaten civil liberties as it looks for patterns in user behavior, sorting though intercepted communications and the Web. The process is used as well to sell you products and services. Data mining is used, for example, by grocery stores to analyze what customers are buying and from that information, to make decisions on what to purchase and where to display the items on the shelves. *See also Customer Relationship Management (CRM).*

Data Quality Act   Act I: Two lobbyist-crafted sentences were slipped into the 2000 appropriations bill—directing the White House Office of Management and Budget to issue guidelines "ensuring and maximizing the quality, objectivity, utility, and integrity of information disseminated by Federal agencies." Act II: John D. Graham, while head of the White House Office of Management and Budget's Information and Regulatory Affairs Office, stated the law will keep the US government hewing to "sound science." The outcome is that a White House official determines what scientific evidence pouring forth from the nation's scientists is valid and what is not. Over 4,000 scientists, including dozens of Nobel laureates and 11 National Medical of Science winners have accused the Bush II Administration of politicizing science through this method. Director of the Environmental Law Clinic, Rena Steinzor, calls the act, "a tool to clobber every effort to regulate." Act III. Companies make use of this law to challenge federal guidelines on fast food diet regulations, timber harvesting on public lands, use of a popular herbicide on American farms but banned by the European Union because it may cause cancer in humans and dropping of TB safeguards. The "sound science" interpretation of scientific data has blocked Environmental Protection Agency scientists from voicing their expert opinion, thus halting implementation of environmental and health regulations. Act IV. In December 2004, a Virginia US district court issued a precedent-setting ruling that will limit the ability of industry groups to allow federal courts to intervene over the validity of federal data, including scientific studies, when the Salt Institute in Washington tangled in court with the prestigious National Institutes of Health's National Heart, Lung and Blood Institute. It seems the Salt Institute did not want this medical body to distribute data regarding the health benefits of a low-sodium diet, basing its lawsuit on the requirements of the Data Quality Act. The OMB Watch, a right-to-know organization, praised the court ruling.

Deaccession   More and more museums appear to be engaged in selling some of their collections to remain alive. This is the far more discreet verb they prefer to describe this activity. In libraries, the Latinate term implies a more professional task than simply weeding obsolete and worn books.

Dead shovel   Hospital emergency room lingo for someone who dies of a heart attack resulting from shoveling snow.

Death tax   The successful campaign waged to eliminate the estate tax by 2009 for all estates valued under $3.5 million became far more widely and politically acceptable once this phrase came into endless repetitive use in public platforms and the media.

Death with dignity   Holding the view that advocates the ending of a person's life when that individual is suffering from severely difficult, disabling and hopeless disease in order to relieve further physical agony. Sometimes this implies withdrawing a treatment that prolongs life. A central issue involves the active ending of a life through assisted suicide or euthanasia administered through a lethal drug injection and at the patient's request. Only in the Netherlands and the State of Oregon is assisted suicide legal.

Debrief   To collect information, or a systematic questioning, often as an oral report, from someone who has been on a military or diplomatic mission, has been held hostage or has worked as a spy or someone who has gone through any other kind of experience of interest to the debriefers. The term grew popular during World War II from the debriefing of pilots and patrols returning from a mission, but is now used to mean, as well, to inform, to brief, as to "debrief the President" on a problem.

Deep ecology   A branch of the environmental movement that believes there is inherent value in all living things and that a nation's thrust to build an industrialized society is fundamentally flawed. They believe the current economic agenda conflicts with the need to nurture the world's animal and plant life towards the goal of a natural ecology of the earth. Those endorsing these ideas plead for a fundamental change in society's values and behavior in order to shape environmental policies that would ensure the preservation of the world's diversity and beauty through compassion for all the planet's communities of living creatures and plant life.

Deep linking   The process of providing a hyperlink allowing a user to seamlessly click over to a Web page other than the site's home page. The controversy related to deep linking is based on whether it is legal for one Web site to link readers to an outside site without the permission of the other site. While deep-linkers view the process as a basic right of the public Internet, opponents of deep linking, often large corporations, offer a variety of reasons for not allowing the process.

Deep six   Once a US Navy term for jettisoning unneeded equipment into the ocean, it took on new meaning with its use by President Nixon's chief domestic affairs adviser, John D. Ehrlichmann, who advised President Nixon's counsel, John Dean, to destroy Watergate evidence.

Defense Department   In 1947, President Harry Truman, not prone to political doubletalk, and his Congress, that was, placed all the US armed forces under a coordinating body called the National Military Establishment. Congressional legislation in 1949 renamed the establishment the Department of Defense. When that occurred, the historic War Department, as old as the Presidency, was reconstituted as the Department of the Army. If President Washington's first Secretary of War were to appear at the Pentagon, it is likely he could not distinguish any difference in mission between his War Department and the present day Defense Department.

Defense spending   Given the Bush II Administration's neocon belief in a first-strike military posture, this term is actually offense spending.

Deficit   When the government spends more than it receives from tax revenues, which used to be vociferously lamented from the right until the George W. Bush Administration made it only mildly troubling to his fellow Republicans. Of course, the impact on the shrinking purchasing power of the in-hock dollar that requires Uncle Sam to borrow $2.1 billion a day from abroad means Americans must work harder and longer to pay for cars, gas and other imported goods.

Degraded   Found in Pentagon press releases during the Second Persian Gulf War, and subsequently repeated, among others, by the Washington Times and the St. Louis Post-Dispatch, the term is a strikingly bureaucratic way of describing the slaughter and dismemberment of huddled Iraqis by shrapnel, concussion bombs and Tomahawk cruise missiles as in, "Republican guard divisions have been ... degraded by US air power."

Dehired   A company dehiring employees is, you guessed it, firing them.

Delayering   A euphemism for reducing the work force by eliminating whole layers of junior or middle management from the organizational structure, but never from the senior levels.

Democracy   To paraphrase Humpty Dumpty's observation to Alice: "When I use the word democracy, it means whatever I want it to mean, neither more nor less." At its best, it offers citizens political choices; at its worst, it becomes an autocratic government's self characterization.

Democratization of status   The means by which through paying a little more for the privilege, anyone can personally demonstrate his affluence. The best illustration comes from selected movie chains that offer such amenities as valet parking and use of private bathrooms to those prepared to hand over the bucks for a premium ticket.

Depopulation   While the word refers to a decrease in population, it can be used in a benign fashion to mean the natural and continuing regional decline in the number of people living in rural farming areas or, as it has been more cynically used in recent years, as a synonym for genocide, the systematic targeting of specific civilian racial, ethnic or religious groups for slaughter and annihilation.

Deselected   Another way of saying you just got fired.

Destination counselor   A travel agent.

Detainees   Political prisoners, popularized by the Republic of South Africa to distinguish anti-apartheid prisoners from common criminals. This is the term used by Bush II's Secretary of Defense, Donald Rumsfeld, to characterize Iraqi prisoners to the Senate Armed Services Committee. Rumsfeld explained they sort prisoner treatment by category: "the President of the United States made a determination in early 2002 that the Geneva Conventions provisions did not apply to our conflict with al Qaeda," although he concluded the Geneva Conventions did apply to the conflict with Taliban. He determined the Taliban detainees did not qualify as prisoners of war under the third Geneva Convention criteria for prisoners of war. He also made "clear" that it was, and will continue to be, the policy to treat detainees humanely and in a manner that is consistent with the Geneva Conventions. Of course, the 2005 report of Vice Admiral Albert Church III said military commanders in Iraq have never been given guidance on handling prisoners in American prison camps. On March 10, 2005, they were, over a year after the prisoner torture at Abu Ghraib came to light. The New York Times noted in a March 11 editorial that the Church report "overlooked Defense Secretary Donald Rumsfeld's approval of interrogation techniques for Guantanamo that violated the Geneva Conventions. It glossed over the way military lawyers who were drafting later rules were ordered to ignore their own legal opinions and instead follow Justice Department memos on how to make torture seem legal, and "Admiral Church and his investigators must have missed the prisoners in hoods, forced into stress positions and threatened by dogs." But as Attorney General Alberto Gonzales has said, if the United States sends a prisoner abroad, then our nation's constitution no longer applies, thus, it's okay to send prisoners to countries where, as the New York Times puts it, "concern for human rights and the rule of law don't pose obstacles to torturing prisoners."

Developing country   Sometimes the phrases are underdeveloped, lesser developed or Third World. But the characteristics of such nations tend to backwardness, poverty, disease and widespread primitive conditions. Many such countries actually grew weaker in the aftermath of the withdrawal of their former colonial occupiers. *See also Underdeveloped, Third World, Lesser Developed*

Dialogue   The term once used simply to connote the spoken words employed in theatrical performances has taken on additional meanings. It now suggests fostering the process of public discourse to shape common understanding in place of conflict within a society, or discussions to bring about peaceful resolution of differences and agreement among different groups or peoples in matters of national, international, cultural or religious affairs.

Dialogue of the deaf   A non-productive exchange of views.

Did you find everything you need?   The automatic greeting of every modern-day cash register clerk, who would likely be annoyed if you in fact gave the person a critique of the marketing options of that particular store, as well as causing eyes to roll of those behind you in the queue.

Dike   In the jargon-filled world of cyberspace, the practice of removing something, such as sections of code; to cut or disable something. *See also Nuke*

Dining room attendant   You may have noticed that this unisex term has long replaced what used to be called a busboy, just as cabin boy has been replaced by the more pleasant-to-the-ears ship's steward.

Directed brokerage   Wall Street pimping, the widespread practice in which stockbrokers accept secret side payments from mutual funds when they steer their unknowing clients into buying shares in the funds.

Dirty driving   The practice of watching a sexually explicit video or DVD while driving, also known as drive-by porn.

Dirty old man   This term is banned as ageist and sexist by the New York City Board of Education in its publications.

Disadvantaged   A sociological or political measure of the degrees of separation between you and those you acknowledge as poor, downtrodden and needy.

Disco rice   New York sanitation workers' slang for maggots.

Dismal science   Thomas Carlyle first scratched this term on paper in 1849 in his *Occasional Discourse on the Negro Question,* attacking "liberal" economists Thomas Malthus and David Ricardo for their support of black emancipation. The world has forgotten Carlyle's perverse argument, and the term has come to characterize economic thought as full of imprecise concepts, and God-knows-what-it-means terms such as indifference curves, multiplier effects and exchange equations.

Dispose in an environmentally correct manner   Please sort your trash into the proper garbage cans.

Dittohead   A term evolving from talk-radio callers, who indicate agreement with the last caller by stating, "Ditto what that last caller said." Its meaning now has three variants: (1) those who espouse the beliefs of Rush Limbaugh heard on his radio talk show; (2) a member of Limbaugh's loyal radio audience albeit one who may not *always* agree with him; and (3) a mindless follower on an issue or idea promulgated by a prominent talking head, politician or cleric.

Do a number To humiliate a person, often without their tracing the action back to you.

Do your own thing What Henry David Thoreau called marching to a different drummer.

Dock worker If discussing *On the Waterfront,* be careful not to use that sexist term, longshoreman, but this term instead.

Document At one time, an important paper of historical or financial import, now any scrap of writing that passes across the desk of a government bureaucrat. Used as a verb, it means to verify with hopefully believable evidence.

Document retention strategy The review and destruction of documents by government functionaries that might prove useful to the media, law enforcement officers or opposition groups, or that would potentially embarrass or reveal illegal activities by government authorities and the functionaries themselves.

Does not compute A term suggesting that the material under consideration has faulty logic or is simply a big fat lie.

Don't ask, don't tell President Clinton, in 1993, asked the Secretary of Defense to draft a policy ending the US military's ban on gay personnel. Much opposition ensued from the Joint Chiefs of Staff, members of Congress, talk show hosts and others. After long debate, President Clinton and the chair of the Senate Armed Services Committee, Senator Sam Nunn, reached a compromise originally called "Don't Ask, Don't Tell, Don't Pursue." That pragmatic solution was codified by Congress in the same year, and remains the law of the land.

Dover factor The idea that Americans lose their resolve for war when they see the bodies of dead soldiers arriving in flag-draped coffins at the US Air Force base in Dover, Delaware. Because American citizens are not thought to have the stomach for a long conflict with a continuous stream of coffins flown stateside,

Pentagon officials defend their ban on news coverage by explaining that this preserves the fallen soldiers' privacy and dignity.

Downsizing   The term configured to appear more acceptable for laying off or firing employees when companies reduce their payrolls to save on expenses and to achieve greater profitability. It doesn't mean reducing the incomes of those who make the decision to slash employment.

Drink the Kool-aid   A term referencing the Jonesville cult mass suicide whereby the members knowingly drank a flavored drink—not really Kool-aid—laced with cyanide. The implication is a true believer in a cause.

Drool-proof paper   Software designers' term for drafting a manual so simple, a vegetable could understand it. This is known as "dumbing down," and such documents often include lawyer-driven statements such as found in an electric toothbrush manual, "a non-functioning unit should no longer be used." *See also Dumbing Down*

DROP (Deferred Retirement Option Program)   This is a plan adopted in the 1990s by a number of municipalities including Houston, Milwaukee and Philadelphia. It was designed to give workers enhanced benefits by allowing them to draw funds from their pension accounts. It was conceived as a way of holding on to employees who were nearing retirement such as teachers or engineers who would be difficult to replace. It was intended to allow such workers to receive large one- time payments upon retirement in addition to their pensions. The consequence, now that the workers are retiring with pensions and retirement incomes greater than the salaries they received while working, is that those cities are staggering under the burden of huge costs they failed to anticipate.

Drop a dime on   What street gang members call the act of informing the police of a criminal act, a snitch.

Drug runs   This is what the trips are called which are made in autos or busses by senior citizens who cross over into Canada or Mexico to fill their prescriptions at lower prices.

Dual commitment   The allegiance to two goals or objectives by following a course of action that simultaneously strives for both.

Instances might include the meritorious Congressional support for National Endowment for the Arts' model programs of indisputable artistic merit while not providing for their wide national public accessibility, or the George W. Bush Administration's zeal in advocating continuous efforts to reduce taxes while driving relentlessly for unrivaled military supremacy.

Dumbing down   While there has always been a choice of personal preferences, dropping by the Globe for Hamlet or next door for a bear-baiting, nowadays the bear-baiting fans have all but closed the Globe. The term in question refers to reducing intellectual content in educational, media, corporate and governmental communications and discourse to the level of the least common denominator. The beauty and original design, speech, product or book has been desiccated, leaving its elegance on the cutting room floor.

Duppies   Having to subsist on unemployment insurance or low pay jobs, young formerly high flyers go by this moniker, short for depressed urban professionals.

Dysfunctional family   In a simpler time, this is what was known as a broken home.

E

Early adopters   The trailblazing individuals who make use of a new technology or other innovative practices long before those with a more cautious wait-and-see personality, by adapting their personal or business behavior to the way they live or work.

Earmarks   Those special stipulations embedded in Congressional bills, allowing for what's left of the cake to be divided only after all the "special" servings are passed out. Sometimes vulgarly termed "giveaways."

Earth muffin   Derisive term, along with Granola Girl, for someone who identifies with the concerns, and often the styles, of the 1960s.

Eastern establishment   The largely mythological clique of formidably potent northeastern and New England financiers, captains of industry and lawyers with common Ivy League roots who once were thought to profoundly influence every White House and Congressional action.

eBay vigilantes   The term for self-appointed monitors of eBay sales, who attempt to halt bogus offers they spot on the site. Their weapons include outbidding credulous buyers with ridiculously high bids or simply alerting the person bidding that they should exercise caution. EBay personnel are not happy to have this assistance, since they have their own security staff to deal with such offers.

Ecospeak   The set of eco-friendly words and phrases which sound right, but serve only as sound bites proffering oversimplified solutions for complicated environmental problems, by dropping them in slogans that veil their bias toward not ruffling the feathers of entrenched business interests.

Economic adjustment   A carousel of bad omens lasting at least two quarters, offering you depressed sales, slowing investment, increased unemployment, growing debt, decreased tax revenues, fewer housing starts, lower factory production and business contraction. A more truthful term would be recession.

Economic deprivation   The plight of being poor dressed up in fancier words.

Economic globalization   Buying, selling and manufacturing everything from food, services and computer products to companies everywhere in the world. Supporters suggest the effect is to raise living standards in the consumer countries that provide an inexpensive work force while increasing the market for goods there. Those opposed decry the loss of jobs in a company's own country to cheap labor abroad by exploiting poor and docile workers who labor under miserable working conditions for pauper wages.

Economically disadvantaged   Still another glossy description for the destitute.

Economy class syndrome   You are squeezed in an airline seat for hours on end, resulting in a clot in a deep vein breaking free and ending up in your pulmonary artery, blocking blood flow to your lungs, with potentially fatal complications. This condition is exacerbated by long six-to-ten-hour flights where you don't get to move around. For most of us who hop across the country in puddle-jumping connecting flights there is much more danger of forgetting your raincoat than experiencing this syndrome.

Educationally challenged   A softer and more politically correct way of describing those who suffer from learning disabilities.

Efficient market hypothesis   A theory that prices in financial markets adjust themselves to reflect every bit of available information about individual businesses, global industries and national economies. And if this be true, it follows that capital markets are remarkably efficient in drawing forth information and allocating needed capital effectively to various activities. This theory contends that securities prices reflect all known information, and that such information is easily and quickly gathered. Thus, it follows that stock prices constantly adjust to their true market value. Recent market history, alas, invalidates that theory; there appears to be a grave lack of omniscience in the marketplace.

Electronic surveillance   A surrogate for the more straightforward word wiretapping.

Eliminate with extreme prejudice   *see*   **Terminate with extreme prejudice**

Elitism   Elitism is mostly in the eye of your banker. Special status and benefits accrue to a privileged class of individuals based upon financial status, level of educational attainment, specialized expert knowledge, inherited class distinctions, prominent family connections, membership in select clubs and organizations or graduation from prestigious institutions. It is often translated into a pattern of snobbish class division built upon inherited privilege and power rather than a more egalitarian system of democratic openness based on merit.

Embarrassing age spots   Another Madison Avenue ploy to not only find something else they want you to worry about on your body, but also to offer a product to conceal it.

Embed   This began as the word for a reporter who remained with the same military unit during coverage of the war in Iraq. Later, the usage expanded to refer to the role of media people covering a candidate's political campaign from start to finish.

Emergency exit light   A US Air Force flashlight.

Emoticons   Those graphic representations of various emotions one finds in emails, such as ☺, now built into software that allow the writer to indicate tongue-in-cheek remarks, outrage and other representations of mood. We now have these icons that substitute what once was done with vocal intonation and the palette of the English language ☹.

Employer mandates   This term surfaced as a key component of the failed health–care initiative by the Clinton Administration in which companies employing a certain number of workers would have been required to buy health insurance for their work force. Since then a number of states have sought to incorporate such employer requirements into their health–care reform efforts, with only Hawaii being successful so far. California, another state in the vanguard of employer mandated health coverage, has passed a law requiring many employers to pay for employees' coverage beginning in 2006. But that law twists in the wind while the courts deliberate whether to overturn it as a result of its being contested by businesses amid claims that the enabling referendum's signatures were improperly collected.

Emotional stereotyping   A major school publisher's guidelines warn against any reference to women as emotional or crying or men being characterized as brave or strong, but it is okay to show men in emotional states and women as brave and strong.

Empowerment   What used to mean obtaining support that would allow any person or a group to break through political, racial or economic barriers. The term has been transformed into a code word for solving the problems of the needy through either self-help or free-market solutions with minimal federal support.

Enabler   Either a person at a workshop, conference or training session who helps move the program along or a person who makes it easier by faulty rationalizations for an alcoholic to continue drinking or an addict's continued use of drugs. In an educational setting, if the enabler is a grade school student he or she is often called by fellow students a teacher's pet; if in college the student is called a suck-up.

Encore TV broadcast   The re-run ad nauseum of previously broadcast television programs.

Energy level   As in high energy level, whereby the former term was hyperactive or frenetic, or low energy level, the former term for which was lazy.

Enemy combatants   A term invented by the Department of Defense for those persons captured by US military forces in the "Afghan theater." The US military does not consider them prisoners of war; thus the guards and interrogators are not constrained by the rules of treatment of prisoners of war agreed upon by the Geneva Conventions. To further evade the footprint of Constitutional protection of basic rights of the accused, approximately 550 of these men are held at the US detention facility at Guantanamo Bay. *See also Extraordinary Rendition*

Engage the enemy on all sides　A Department of Defense term for ambush.

Enhanced interrogation techniques　CIA term for feigned drowning, "stress positions," light and noise bombardment, sleep deprivation and other methods used in interrogation of al Qaeda leaders. Formerly approved by the White House, until they were suspended after media coverage of the abuses scandal of Abu Ghraib prison in Iraq.

Enhanced radiation device　This is what the Pentagon called a neutron bomb in a Congressional budget submission.

Enlightened self interest　The belief that if you push on one end of a balloon, it will not swell elsewhere. Studies reveal that middle- and lower-income Americans support tax cuts. These tax cuts go largely to the rich, but the rest of us figure we will benefit as well, only to a lesser degree. No one makes the connection that without the big bucks coming in from taxing the rich, the cupboard will be bare, and your schools and roads and police and libraries, to name a few government services, will have less operating funds. Thus, your children will have less effective schooling, your car will hit more potholes, there will be less law enforcement, and your branch library will close. See the connection? It is the first law of municipal thermodynamics.

Entitlements　While this is traditionally used to characterize the benefits received by workers from their employers and part of their overall compensation and incentive package, or in having taxes taken from wages for purposeful benefits such as unemployment insurance, in more recent parlance it has come to be used more and more in a derogatory sense as a synonym for welfare or other government social programs.

Episode　A bureaucratic term used by governments and power companies to indicate a hazardous condition resulting in illness and death due to excessive pollution discharge or radiation leaks.

Equal opportunity The term was originally applied to affirmative action programs that were designed to afford equal access to schools, jobs and housing by offering the same opportunities to those restricted by social, religious or gender discrimination. In more recent years it has been assaulted both rhetorically and in litigation by those feeling aggrieved because they view themselves as unjustly denied their equal rights. They reason that they, members of the majority that has enjoyed all the traditional advantages, are now victimized by affirmative action measures.

Erectile dysfunction Medical advertising expression for the inability of a man to perform sexually.

Eternity leave Compensated absence provided by compassionate companies to employees who take care of those dear to them during a terminal sickness.

Ethnic cleansing Murdering men, women and children who are members of religious or social groups held in disfavor by another religious or social group. The phrase implies racial purification, rather than the more honest term genocide.

Eve and Adam The American Philosophical Association's guidelines for non-sexist terms suggest this realignment.

Event A government and industrial term used to describe accidents in a nuclear plant.

Evidence free A polite term for lie used by David Kay, former head of the CIA's Iraq Survey Group, to characterize Vice President Cheney's claim—backed up by Bush II—that Saddam Hussein maintained longstanding ties to al Qaeda.

Evil biology Besides weapons of mass destruction, former Attorney General John Ashcroft warned of this new danger in January 2004 shortly after David Kay, top weapons inspector in Iraq, stated he did not believe weapons of mass destruction existed in Iraq. Ashcroft suggested that if Saddam Hussein had not been overthrown, his astrolabs might have turned to "evil chemistry and evil biology."

Exactly This word is heard repeatedly in conversations these days, expressed each time someone offers an opinion, no matter how ludicrous. In bygone days, it was used to indicate you were following the discussion with at least a modicum of interest or agreement, meaning, "I tend to agree," or the more neutral, "I see."

Exceptional   Used to describe children with disabilities, often mental retardation.

Excessive volatility   A Panglossian concept used by the Bush II Treasury Secretary John W. Snow, referring to the once strong dollars exchange rate against currencies such as the Euro. Secretary Snow posits the Administration's plunging dollar rate is swell since that helps sell American goods to foreign markets, and allows for higher employment to make those non-cheapened goods. Of course, a weaker dollar means the American consumer will have to shell out more to buy imported goods—cars, gas, consumer electronics and clothes, and Uncle Sam (read taxpayer) will need to borrow billions more at higher interest rates. But at least the dollar is not exhibiting volatility; it just keeps sinking like a lead plug.

Exhausted   Not only used for the physically fatigued—this refers to workers who reach the end of the term covered by their state unemployment insurance when their benefits are used up.

Exit strategy   A term long used in the stock market referring to the preplanned liquidation or repayment of investments, and now a common term for the complex of preparation and support for the evolving government, infrastructure rebuilding, political restructuring, and military withdrawal in Iraq. Critical consensus has been that the entry strategy was well planned and the exit strategy is a case study in ineptitude by the Bush II Administration.

Expensing stock options   The practice by which publicly owned companies place a fair market value on the stock options that they distribute to their managers or employees and include that information along with other compensation costs on the corporate balance sheet that they provide to stockholders and the Securities and Exchange Commission. The Financial Accounting Standards Board, the body that holds its mandate from the SEC, has produced a precise rule for such reporting after many years of preparation. However, Congress is being pressured by many business interests, notably the high tech firms, to block the enforcement of that rule since these companies argue that they rely heavily on stock options to attract and keep employees, and the rule would be unfair to them. But if options are not treated in a transparent way exactly like other compensation charges, investors and analysts cannot easily recognize how options relate to a company's profitability. For the final outcome, stay tuned.

Expert   Specialist engaged by company or government managers to deliver an opinion on a problem facing the organization. Very often the advice dexterously confirms the views about the solution held by those who retained the consultant.

Expletive   Popularized by the transcripts of the Nixon White House Watergate tapes, in which "expletive deleted" became a recurring refrain, used to indicate profanity.

Extended constructed response   This was universally called composition in an earlier and simpler time in secondary education.

Extensions   Someone else's hair or synthetic hair braided or sewn onto our own for fuller body and length.

Extremist   Anyone whose thinking about a current government policy is different from the prevailing position. *See also Controversial*

Extraordinary rendition   The Bush II Administration's name for outsourcing of torture by using US agents to take alleged terrorists to countries outside the footprint of US legislation—and its umbrella of rights for the accused—to a country where the prisoner is preyed upon by trained tormentors. Rendition was used on a limited basis before September 11, 2001 for persons with outstanding arrest warrants, but was expanded to an estimated 150 persons, prisoners who had never been charged with a crime in a court of law, but who are simply "illegal enemy combatants." Jane Mayer, in a February 14, 2005, New Yorker article writes that "the most common destinations for rendered suspects are Egypt, Morocco, Syria and Jordan, all of which have been cited for human rights violations by the State Department and are known to torture suspects." The New York Times reported on March 6, 2005, that "several former detainees have described being subjected to coercive interrogation techniques and brutal treatment during months spent in detention under the program in Egypt and other countries." After the alleged kidnapping in Milan on February 17, 2003, of suspected terrorist Hassan Mustafa Osama Nasr, also know as Abu Omar, 13 CIA operatives were named in a warrant issued by Italian judge Guido Salvini, since their action violated Italian sovereignty and disrupted an Italian police investigation. Nasr was flown to Egypt for interrogation. In June 2005, the Italian government summoned the US ambassador to discuss the 2003 abduction and denied that it authorized the alleged CIA-led kidnapping.

Eye candy   The hip tastemakers who set the style in dress and demeanor in the frenetic world of New York's late late hour dance clubs. Also a term of approval, often used by gays, for attractive models.

Eyes only   A high security classification used by the State Department meaning the message should only be read by the addressee. Given how such messages are distributed overseas and within the State Department and the forbidden-fruit appeal of such classification, such messages are sure to be read by a host of individuals at both ends of the transmission.

F

Fabrication   A Latinate way of indicating a lie.

Face time   The term refers to an ancient mode of communication when speakers are in each other's presence, exchanging thoughts without electronic assistance. In media land, it's the time actually spent before a live camera. In law, trade shows and accounting firms the term refers to the time spent in direct personal interaction.

Facility   Besides its use to mean toilet, it replaces that useful term building in athletics, stadium or ball park; and among jailers it replaces prisons with correctional facilities.

Fact   An assertion that is endlessly repeated by a political party or advocacy group until leaked information or a Freedom of Information release disproves it.

Faction   The designation for a magazine piece or book in which a fictional component has been added to a factual base.

Failure to launch   The inability, through lack of initiative, significant unpaid student loans or joblessness, of those in their twenties and sometimes early thirties to move out of the parents' residence.

Fair trade   Think this means business fairness? Wrong: it is exactly the reverse. It is the strategy used by manufacturers to avoid competition by requiring distributors to sell their goods for a set amount without special sales prices or discounts, thereby fixing prices in restraint of trade.

Family values   Exactly what this means is clear only to the person using this term and those people nodding their head in agreement. Here is a helpful checklist. Take your pick: virginity until marriage, raising children, obeying the law, paying taxes and living according to traditional religious beliefs. Or maybe it means unswerving loyalty to the family at any cost. This soft and fuzzy term is loved by politicians, who know voters will embrace it like a treasured teddy bear.

Fast track authority *see* **Trade promotion authority**

Fat   When not used to characterize excess poundage in individuals, the word is a favorite of politicians who endlessly excoriate the condition in lamenting the extravagant level of resources they find in the budgets and expenditures of government agencies and programs that are not their favorites.

Fear up harsh   Military intelligence terminology for significantly increasing the fear level in a security detainee by using whatever methods are deemed necessary to make him believe that his only hope in life is to divulge whatever information the interrogator is seeking.

Federally impacted area   The way local governments describe a locale where there are a great many government non-taxpaying institutions; as for example, a military base. Supplying schooling and other services to these local non-taxpaying residents traumatizes the community's tax base.

Female empowered adult education   Term for the growing cadre of women entrepreneurs selling sex to other women in the form of adult Web sites, stores, catalogs and toy products. These businesses treat sex and love from a woman's perspective and the varied fare on the Internet includes porno plots, foreplay and aftermath cuddling. Customers are both heterosexuals and lesbians and the trade is especially mindful of female tastes, suggesting new ways for women to find pleasure.

Feminazis   Employed by anti-feminists to denigrate activists who militate for women's rights and just treatment.

Feminist   Used as a badge of honor or derogatorily to characterize those individuals assuming an overly aggressive stance for promoting equal rights and free choice for women.

Feng Shui   Now permeating contemporary lifestyles, this is the 8,000-year-old-Chinese concept of allowing a positive energy to flow through your home, work space and interior furnishings. The idea, combining the Chinese characters for wind and water, is to live in harmony with your environment so that the cosmic universal cycles work best with your living spaces. In the West, the concept was first popularized by interior designers and architects to lead to spiritual serenity and, in the business world, financial success. The popular press caught up with the process, suggesting its might not only lead to lowered stress levels but even to a more rewarding love life.

Feral cities   A term coined by scholar Richard J. Norton for a city of over a million in population that has lost its government structure, is without basic utilities, suffers from rampant corruption, lacks city health and security support, contains high levels of disease and has ceded control of the various neighborhoods administered by armed groups. Norton suggests several cities are approaching this stage, including parts of Mexico City, Karachi, San Paulo and Johannesburg. Among the many dangers is that these cities are likely to draw terrorist organizations.

Financial advisor   High-flown phrase for securities or insurance salespeople.

Financial services   This is what businesses that offer credit or make small loans predominantly to the poor at exorbitant rates call themselves.

Financial underachiever   Another way to demean the indigent.

Finishing school   Young women of refinement drawn from the elite class once attended secondary schools with this appellation, dedicated to preparing their students for future social lives and responsibilities by emphasizing cultural studies and accomplishments, thereby grooming them for matrimonial roles. The term now is used pejoratively to characterize lightweight academic programs for females.

First-strike capability   The nation's capability to deliver a military blow to an enemy that would be so deadly as to destroy the ability of the enemy to retaliate. This differs from a pre-emptive strike, which would carry out an assault in the face of any perceived threat first, before an enemy's power grows, but it is not viewed to be so devastating in destructive effect.

Fixer-upper   A real estate term meaning the house is in shambles, and no respectable agent would show it to you without that warning.

Flash mobs   A fad that has caught on in recent months is the coming together of suddenly formed Internet gatherings that group around all kinds of end objectives. One such group, a large volunteer collective of students, will network their joint computing capability to resemble a supercomputer.

Flip flop   A political label indicating indecisiveness. In a 2004 Republican TV ad, a sound-bite of the silly term flip flop played while we watched a clip of Democrat John Kerry tacking from side to side on a windsurfer, the Blue Danube waltz emphasizing the sail snaps. Kerry was portrayed as the antithesis of a leader; irresolute and driven by external forces. This was followed by ads aired in the Midwest with the flop-flop sound bite while showing a weathervane spinning about. As a result, the real issues of the campaign were overlooked. As print journalists often noted, President Bush, through political necessity, had abandoned a multitude of positions on issues such as the merits of creating a Homeland Security Department, tariffs on steel, air pollution regulation, nation-building, and whether states should be allowed to sanction same-sex marriage.

Flyover land   A term of derision characterizing the area of continental US that lies between the West Coast and the Northeast, dismissed as a cultural wasteland by sophisticated travelers on their cross-country flights.

Foggy Bottom   Facetious way of referring to the Department of State either because of the obscurity of its official language or because its Washington, DC headquarters sits atop what was once a swamp.

Folk wisdom   A term the American Psychological Association suggests replace old wives' tales.

For your convenience   When you hear any business describing its procedures or practices in this way, you just know it is for their convenience, not yours.

Force flow   In military jargon, this identifies how well supply lines keep up or fall behind in moving at the pace of combat forces.

Foreign professional guest workers   This is a type of on-shore out-sourcing described in the language of the World Trade Organization as "the movement of natural persons" and is considered to be a form of trade in services. It results in provisions for providing a greatly increased number of temporary visas for such individuals—more than 865,000 in 2003. And it makes it easier for American companies, universities and hospitals to hire such employees, typically at much lower salaries than they would pay for American workers. In some fields, such as nursing and computer programming, the influx of workers is substantial enough to lower wages and reduce benefits for American rivals. While the visas are called temporary, some 100,000 guest workers annually apply for and receive permanent res-idence—the so-called green cards.

Forests with a future   A slogan coined for the US Forest Service by its PR firm, One World Communications. The watchword is part of the Forest Service's 2004 Sierra Nevada forest management plan, which will triple commercial logging and allow larger trees to be cut in national forests. This will, in the words of the Forest Service, "reduce overstocked forest conditions and potential insect and disease prob-lems." They have a point; you can't have forest insect infestation if you remove the forest.

Fragging   The language for murdering officers or non-commis-sioned officers by fragmentation grenades tossed into their locations by their own soldiers. It came into use first during the Vietnam War and was often attributed, rightly or wrongly, to the influence of nar-cotics on the soldiers who perpetrated it.

Free market   The prevailing sentimental value of political conser-vatives when, in actuality, it is the last thing that business truly wants since it would make it necessary to seriously compete, reduce prices, perennially innovate, suffer narrower profit margins and be at constant risk of possible bankruptcy. Big business much prefers ensured profits, monopoly control, price supports and trade protec-tions and other elements of a corporate welfare state. What large scale firms adore most are the tax and regulatory loopholes and sub-sidies that put them at a distinct advantage over current or potential competitors.

Free trade   Unrestricted and uncontrolled access to markets in an international economic system without tariffs or import or export controls between or among member nations. Opponents reason that this is merely a way to encourage American manufacturers to move factories to other lands to take advantage of cheap labor, thereby causing increased unemployment in the US and imbalances of trade. This is what the mounting public protests against the free trade activities of the World Trade Organization are all about.

Free world   A hackneyed political slogan for that group of nations whose sympathies are allied to American interests, whether their citizens enjoy freedom or are ruled by despots.

Freedom car   The term for automobiles to be powered by "free fuel" as part of a George W. Bush Administration initiative intended to ulti-mately develop a hydrogen-fueled car. The unspoken feature of the program is how car manufacturers remain off the hook for making needed improvements in fuel efficiency that would reduce American dependence on oil imports and thereby lessen the dan-gers of global warming as well as lowering commute costs. Fuel effi-ciency of cars has dropped to a 21-year low, influenced by SUV jug-gernauts; there are no deadlines or enforceable milestones to actual-ly deliver a hydrogen-fueled car.

Freedom deficit   The political characterization of foreign govern-ments which are on friendly terms with the US but behave despoti-cally by repressing their own populations.

Freedom fries   What populist politicos in Congress pressured their cafeteria to term french fries, after the French turned down Bush II's request for armed forces to join his Iraqi hunt for weapons of mass destruction. However, this appellation stops at the crest of Capitol Hill. For example, at the Palm Restaurant, typically awash in lobbyists succoring members of Congress, french fries are called just that.

Fresh to death   Clothing termed thusly in the hip hop fashion world is so hot that it will stay cool to wear until the owner is long dead.

Friendly fire   Regardless of what the military says about being hit by bombs or shells by one's own side, it is the result of incompetence, not friendly feelings toward those targeted.

Front-end load   Not an automotive term, but a sales charge you pay when you first buy a mutual fund or similar investment. This is different from the usual mutual fund that catches up with you later for its "administrative expenses and transaction costs." It has occurred to mutual fund managers that if you pay for this fee up front, you might be hesitant to jump to another fund, where you would have to start the process all over again.

Full employment   This does not mean that everyone who wants a job is employed. Rather it is a benchmark used by economists when about 4 percent of the work force is without jobs, and thus the nation's economy is described as enjoying full employment.

Full waisted   A term used by haberdashers in lieu of fat or potbellied. Trousers are "cut fuller in the waist."

Furlough   Unless one is in the armed forces, no happy associations are enjoyed by this unwanted holiday from work when people are being laid off.

Further study   A surefire tactic by the Executive Branch as well as the Congress to evade the action needed on pressing problems by commissioning an investigation.

The 411   The Southern Baptist Convention proselytizing its evangelical gospel message to sinners in New York City in a two-year campaign begun in 2004. The 411 designation is from I Peter 4:11, celebrating the glory of God.

Gaming   Rather than resort to the earthier gambling, this is the label of choice used by jurisdictions disposed to encourage or simply tolerate the practice of betting.

Gaming the system   Using that maze of complexity found in government regulations to drain off funds, money that finds its way into your own wallet or that of your company. Recent examples include overcharging Medicare patients through use of fabricated diagnosis and complex billing codes, and the UN oil-for-food scandal.

Gate rape   The language used by members of air crews to describe how they are too frequently subjected to random searching by security personnel when headed for their flight departures because they can't register any objection for fear of being punished.

Gated community   While this may be slang for prison, a present day gated community continues the medieval castle-building concept of protection from marauders and miscreants. It is unfortunate, therefore, that many are not totally fenced, and expect today's sneak-thief to kindly stop at the main gate and be refused a pass.

Gen X   Used by pundits to categorize Americans born between 1961 and 1981, stereotypically independent minded, lacking in commitment, questioning of various forms of authority and deeply mistrustful of traditional institutions. *See also Baby Boomers*

Gen Y   The 78 million offspring of either baby boomers or Gen X, they have not as yet reached the big 3 oh. From infancy, they have learned your remote can click to a reality of your choice, that mama is just a cell-phone page away, and you pay for groceries with a credit card. Their characteristics as a cohort are still evolving, but the common experience of four hours a day of television watching has nurtured a breed that demands flexibility, and constant stimulation, and disdainfully eyes those who grab the job-and-family strap of the wage slave. Their social life and work often blend together. They have always known the threat of AIDS, crack and terrorist attacks, spend more on clothes than housewares, have an average $3,000 debt on their credit cards, are computer literate, multi-tasking, adaptable, team-oriented, and as a group have around $140 billion in disposable income. They are increasingly spending that money online.

Generation O   Used to characterize the masses of present day kids who are significantly obese.

Generica   The creeping sprawl into the suburbs of American cities that devours open space, destroys the unique character of a region with its ubiquitous sameness and contributes to urban decay and the crumbling of the residential core of once vibrant cities, whose residents have vanished.

Genetic pollution   This has recently become a common term in the environmental movement and is increasingly turning up in newspaper reports. It was popularised by the American environmental campaigner Jeremy Rifkin in his book *The Biotech Century*, published in May 1998. He used the term for the risk that genes from genetically modified organisms (*GMOs* in the jargon) could be dispersed as a result of their breeding with wild relatives or even with unrelated species. Since genetically modified plants include resistance to control sprays, one result could be that weeds will become resistant to herbicides or pesticides, becoming, in other words of the moment, *superweeds* that are *supercompetitive*. The worst case is that such transformed species could spread widely, take over other habitats, and force rare or vulnerable wild species into extinction. This is one basis for the great controversy in Britain at the moment over genetically modified crops, which has led to calls for a moratorium on their introduction.

Genius of capitalism   The term used by Bush II's former Treasury Secretary Paul O'Neil in explaining the sudden collapse of the house of cards known as Enron; a sort of "these things happen" explanation, with O'Neil expounding that "people get to make good decisions or bad decisions, and they get to pay the consequence or to enjoy the fruits of their decisions. That's the way the system works." Of course, the Enron brass padlocked the company after first cleaning out its bank account, leaving the rest of us holding the bag.

Genuine imitation leather   Possibly the advertiser means the leather is imitation, but has a warm, open personality.

Geographical chauvinism   Since the United States shares the North American continent with other countries, an educational test publisher asks its writers to avoid using the term American foreign policy or American economic gains, but instead, substitute US for American.

Get a life!   A not-so-subtle suggestion heard from friends or associates of obsessive workers, over-serious email forum contributors, computer geeks, and those students who consistently score higher grades than you by the unfair practice of putting in more hours of study. Star Trek's William Shatner used this phrase on his legendary *Saturday Night Live* sketch and repeated it as the title of his autobiography.

Get your ticket punched   A management practice in which to rise through the ranks in the military, foreign service or many professions, you must take on specific activities and assignments. In the military, it requires commanding a ship or land-based group as well as receiving a ribbon for serving in an armed conflict; in the foreign service, to reach ambassador you need to have served as both a Washington–based desk officer as well as an embassy political officer.

Getting along   If someone observes you are getting along, they are trying to avoid saying you are old.

Getting it together   Often followed by "for a successful (blank) experience" or "to overcome your (blank) problem;" in either case the idea is to address an issue in an organized, possibly "more mature" manner.

Ghetto bird   Hip hop for police helicopter.

Globophobe   Description of one who resists or feels threatened by globalization trends.

God-sponsored violence   The Middle Eastern states, including Israel and the West Bank and Gaza, have become the most recent epicenters of this form of bloodshed

God's will   The divine sanctification of any form of political, military or personal choice for actions taken.

Golden handcuffs   A financial incentive paid to an employee that is so advantageous that it discourages the person from leaving the company. Also, persons who hang on to dreadful positions for fear of losing their health benefits.

Golden handshake   The staggering severance compensation given to an about-to-retire corporate chieftain.

Golden parachute   The astoundingly bountiful severance and compensation packages with which corporate titans reward themselves at the expense of their shareholders when their companies are merged or sold and their personal reigns of power and authority end.

Google Darwinism   Fat-beaked finches observed by Darwin could survive without computer-driven algorithms, but for those savvy survivors who want to see their Web sites appear near the top of Google searches have calculated a strategy for exploiting Google's logic for getting results, spelling survival.

Gorelet   This was the moniker given to the water-conserving toilet that features low-flow double flushing that was recommended when President Clinton and Vice President Gore were in office.

Government interference   The furry nose of government pushing under the private enterprise tent via laws, regulations and oversight activities, thus interfering with what business people and industrialists see as incursions into their operations. The alternative is for business to set its own standards of conduct and to implement measures to address customer concerns and trade practices and to protect the health and safety of its employees.

Government relations specialist   Someone who plies his trade as a lobbyist in the halls of Congress, using connections, favors, guile and sometimes even facts in seeking to influence legislators, regulators and bureaucrats on behalf of his or her clients and their interests. Often a well-paying sanctuary for politicians departed from office.

Grade Inflation   The practice by college professors of awarding students a higher grade than their performance in a course is really worth. Some trace the phenomenon back to the Vietnam war period when instructors were loathe to give low grades that might have led to students failing and thereby becoming eligible for the draft. In later years when academic institutions began to view their students as customers paying considerable sums for tuition, this sentiment resulted in striving for customer satisfaction. The practice has become so widespread in spite of its heated denial by many colleges that a number of institutions, including some of the most prestigious Ivy League schools, are seeking to restore grading standards of the past when an A signified excellent achievement.

Granola girl *see* **Earth muffin**

Grantsmanship   The skill of knowing where the money is to make it possible to receive support to carry out programs that precisely match the donor's interests.

Grassroots   Those home folks who can be counted upon to support the prejudices and bias of their elected representative.

Grassroots blogs   A new entry in the history of American elections comes about with this term. Just as our eyes start to roll at all those political ads on television, this term appears, meaning a personal blog devoted to spreading the word, good or bad, about a political candidate. As Howard Dean proved in his run for the Democratic nomination for President in 2004, you can't connect to a political constituency by broadcast, but blogs are "narrowcasting" with a punch. For not only do they provide information about the candidate but they actively involve the reader to write something in response, which engages the person in the issues.

Gray economy   Unpaid work done within families or communities as a result of informal arrangements between neighbors and friends, estimated to result in almost half the value of work carried out in the formal economy.

Grayback   Educator's term referencing the elder members of their faculty who, like aging great apes, have power in the department, but are rigid, lack interest in new educational innovations and fight needed changes.

Graylisting   The practice in which networks and radio stations seek to censor the broadcast of music they view as questionable due to unpatriotic or suggestive content that might be offensive to their listening audience.

Great man theory   The idea that significant events are profoundly influenced by the actions or persuasive pronouncements by certain leaders of government or business because of their charismatic leadership qualities.

Great Society   Term used by Lyndon Johnson to dramatize his aspirations in advancing the social welfare and racial legislation initiatives in the 1960s. The phrase was not original; it was used as a book title in 1914 by Graham Wallas.

Greedy geezers   A term coined by writer Henry Fairlie, suggesting that the senior lobby is getting out of hand. At present, conservative attacks on special interests for the elderly are gunning for the largest oldster lobbying group in the world, AARP, because AARP is fighting the Bush II plan to privatize Social Security. The anti-AARP forces are led by USA Next, a far-right group noted for their Swift-boat ads attacking John Kerry.

Greenfields   The term is used in two ways. First, it is used to describe new housing and commercial tracts sometimes with the local municipality taking it upon itself to supply the electricity, natural gas and other utilities in competition with big investor-owned utilities. The other definition is when former brownfields (see definition) are converted to clean new parkland, residential and commercial space. Greenfields often provide desperately needed urban open space serving inner-city dwellers.

Greenwash   Environmental public relations masking a company's real environmental practices and policies, thus deflecting criticism from committed greens.

GU   A coy acronym reportedly adopted by what used to be called the dating set to indicate an otherwise desirable person who lives too far away, i.e., geographically undesirable.

Guilt-free vacationing The enlightened organizational directive clearly suggesting that their employees refrain from carrying with them during their holidays all their electronic connections like cell phones, pagers and portable computers so that they can resist the urge to constantly check back with the office.

Gun control The right to "keep and bear arms" was appended to the US Constitution by the Founding Fathers because they remembered that the former rulers of the territory had tried to disarm them to subdue their rebellion and that they were still living among Native Americans or lawless individuals who, for a variety of reasons, were hostile. Our armed government forces, military, and police have subdued the last of the Native American rebellions, and criminals continue to be confronted by deputized police. Thus, the gun control issue comes down to what level of personal protection, rather than deputized protection is required, unless you live in Idaho and like to dress up in camouflage gear and pretend you are a militia group protecting your land from jack-booted government thugs, as the National Rifle Association defines this threat. Meanwhile medical authorities and our delegated protectors, the police, tell us the real hostiles are ourselves, pistol-packing papas shooting tardy daughters, mistaking them for intruders, or small children playing with these lethal toys, blowing holes in their hard-to-repair bodies. Your local deputy sheriff, you may notice, now wears a bulletproof vest, hoping that the right-to-bear-arms criminal, who is planning to shoot the sheriff, does not aim for the head and uses less than armor-piercing bullets. It is an ongoing conflict of rights between the quality of life and whom you distrust the most. In the US, this present mix of opposing forces, and our need for hobbyist hunting means that every hour, four people die by gunshot, every 54 hours a police officer is killed, and annually over 4,000 children are sacrificed.

Hackademy   Schooling those with a penchant for illegally hacking into computer systems.

Hacktivism   This is the process of using the techniques of hackers for a social or political purpose, by targeting an institution's Web site or its internal information networks. It is, like hacking, illegal, but it is practiced with a sort of Robin Hood attitude against the biggies. Hacktivists' activities include defacing or disabling a Web site and inserting various kinds of viruses. Some political hacktivists appear to have close connections to their respective governments, as illustrated by the attacks on Chinese and American Web sites in 2001 when a Chinese fighter collided with a US Navy spy plane over the South China Sea.

Hair disadvantaged   Used to assuage the tender feelings of the bald.

Hajis   In much the same way that American troops referred to the native population in Vietnam as "gooks," this is the derisive expression used by the military for indigenous Iraqis.

Handcrafted   A term often reinforced with "one-of-a-kind" or "cuddly" that has an inverse relationship to those products of knowledgeable craftspeople whose art and skill do not need this desperate descriptor.

Handicapism and handicapped   Handicapism is defined as discrimination toward those with disabilities, including use of stereotypes. Also, the term denigrates remarks such as "blind as a bat." Also banned by many textbook publishers is the term handicapped, or handicapped person, with the suggested replacement being "a person with a disability."

Hard line Members of the far right who believe they alone "face facts" about America's challenges and have the guts to take action. They see America's overwhelming military and economic power as a kind of Theodore Roosevelt Big Stick. But ignoring Teddy's admonition to "speak softly," they want to put that stick to use to batter down obstacles to American primacy. Past battle-cries: better, more plentiful nukes not wimpy "arms control;" victory in Vietnam not a "negotiated peace," escalate the Vietnam war into Cambodia, Laos and North Vietnam; eliminate the Sandinistas in Nicaragua and mine the harbors there; to hell with the United Nations, assault all nations that use "terror as a weapon;" and like Lenny and his rabbit farm, believe that weapons of mass destruction are still to be found in Iraq.

Hardcore Prefacing pornography, it indicates a triple x version; used with believer, the term indicates a passionate refusal to consider alternative explanations. For example, one who despite all the scientific evidence to the contrary believes flying saucers are landing in New Mexico or weapons of mass destruction could still be unearthed in occupied Iraq.

Hardware Since we have computer software, can hardware be far behind? In the Cold War era, the term was modified by "military," meaning armaments like tanks and missiles, but now is stuff you get at a computer store that usually has rebates and serial numbers and provides services that are better than your last upgrade, but costs more.

Harvest Furriers talk of harvesting seals or sables, deer hunters use the term in preference to shooting or killing.

Have a good one A replacement for "good afternoon," "good day" or "good evening," used in more gracious times.

Have sex The contemporary form of expression for a male and female engaging in some form of sexual intercourse, popularized by President Clinton's statement, "I did not have sex with that woman."

Having a relationship   The term often has an unstated modifier such as "intimate" or "inappropriate."

Hazardous waste   Perhaps it sounds less dire but it is just as lethal as the term it often is evading, nuclear waste.

He doesn't get it   A derisive description of someone who has not kept up with the changing times, particularly those who retain sexist attitudes.

Headcount reduction   You can tell your kids that you were not fired, just part of a headcount reduction.

Health care facility   What was once a medical building or doctor's office has been transformed into a health care facility.

Healthy forests   Bush II, in 2003, signed the Orwellianly misnamed "Healthy Forests Initiative," a clear-cutting of environmental regulations for our national forests, regulations that had evolved from many previous Administrations. In 2004, a week before Christmas—a favorite time for Administrations to stick it to a distracted public—the Forest Service published a fundamental revision of the rules governing the nation's national forests. The reason given for the radical changes was to streamline management and to provide greater autonomy to local managers. But the baby was thrown out with the bathwater. The new rules eliminate needed environmental reviews, requirements mandated by the National Environmental Policy Act of 1969, delimit public input, and replace detailed regulations, as the *New York Times* notes, "like those limiting clearcuts and protecting streams, with vague 'results-based' goals." Conservationists deplore the fact that wildlife preservation and recreation are no longer considered the foremost criteria for managing national forests. Instead, logging and other commercial activities will be given equal importance ostensibly to keep the forests "healthy." These changes, the *New York Times* states, "open an enormous acreage to tree harvesting, road construction and mechanized logging. Those intrusions can cause severe erosion and threaten water quality." The initiative also weakens the environmental review process—once routinely required by land management agencies—and your rights to contest forest management plans in court. The New York Times pointed to still another problem with the new rules: "Forest supervisors have always been subject to fierce pressures from timber companies and the communities that depend upon them for jobs." Former legal requirements removed, local industry pressures likely will decide the forests' future.

Hearts and minds   A catchphrase associated with government-led programs to garner the support of local populations, often armed insurgents. The term first became popular in the 1950s when the British Army attempted to subdue the Communist guerrillas of Malaya. After failed results using World War II battlefield strategies, the British Army changed its tactics "to win the hearts and minds," with a decentralized organization and doctrinal flexibility, free primary schooling for all the ethnic groups in the country, working with the local soon-to-be-independent government and the subordination of the military to the political. The process worked in Malaya, contrasted with neighboring Vietnam, where former West Point instructor John Nagl posits the US Army actively resisted the adaptations necessary to counter insurgent warfare.

Helicopter parents   The generation Y kids never heard "go out and play," having grown up with a full calendar of arranged play, from t-ball to soccer to piano lessons, and with a parent hovering nearby to keep tabs and provide a shield of steady encouragement, much like a protective tariff, insulating them from the dog-eat-dog competition of the real world. Now the oldest members of the generation Y are leaving that protective cover for the world of work and are finding that their boss is a lot more demanding than those soft pitch games of yesteryear; no more trophies to take home just for showing up.

Heteroflexible   Adolescent jargon for those engaging in other than the typical manner of male-female sexual behavior.

Heterosexist   The personal or civil assumption that everyone is heterosexual, or, by God, should be.

Hexiform rotatable surface compression units   What the US Navy calls a steel nut.

Hide and sleep weapons   A new form of military weaponry which remains dormant on a battlefield or surreptitiously enters an enemy area and is not activated until a distant target comes into view, at which point it fires.

High fratricide levels   This is a Pentagon term that refers to an unacceptable level of blowing up one's own missiles, tanks and aircraft, usually caused by inadequate time for the person using the weapon to decide if the target is friend or foe, or because the weapon was programmed incorrectly or the electronic targeting equipment malfunctioned.

High maintenance person   A term for one who requires a great deal of assistance in all aspects of life, be they demanding, neurotic or simply clueless.

Highlight   In political parlance, pointing to an instance or data that support your point of view, distracting the audience from the true facts of the case.

Hikikomori   While American teenagers are more known for never being home, this imported term is used for withdrawn, often friendless Japanese youth who, hermit-like, spend all their time in their bedrooms, often living a reverse schedule of sleeping during the day and watching TV or playing video games at night; preferring a virtual reality life to the real thing—with school pressures apparently one triggering factor. This may be a passing phase or last for months or years, and is estimated to impact at least a million young people in Japan. Social workers and the courts rarely get involved if they refuse to attend school, but increasingly, clinics are offering help for this problem.

Histrionic personality disorder   Even in this age of political correctness, it seems more satisfying, somehow, to use the older terms: a megalomaniac bastard or a neurotic bitch.

Hockey dad   A suburban male's counterpart to a soccer mom, made famous by former Presidential candidate Howard Dean's self-description following his screaming episode in the aftermath of the Iowa Democratic presidential primary debacle.

Holistic   Looking at the entirety rather than parts of the whole: in medicine viewing the body as a system, with spiritual, mental, emotional and physical parts; in an ecosystem, looking at the whole, since the view is the components cannot be separated from their parts. It is difficult to find a self-help book that is devoid of this term.

Hollywoodize   A media term referencing the recent insertion of tabloid topics, such as breathless accounts of glitterati weddings and the foibles of rock stars, into a news broadcast intended to attract a younger "demographic." The term can also mean the destruction of a well known book by scriptwriters to allow the story to be squeezed into Hollywood formulas.

Home   What used to be a house. Now, contractors build homes, you borrow money with a home improvement loan, but thankfully "under home arrest" and "boardinghome reach" have not caught on.

Homemade   A term whose original meaning is all but lost, and all one can hope for is that the homemade apple pie you order is made in the same city in which the restaurant is located. The term has been on a long slide downhill, however: Governor George Hunt, the beloved first governor of the State of Arizona, used to hand out to favored constituents jars of homemade jam as fast as his wife could steam the A & P labels off.

Home English   One major textbook publisher asks its authors to not mention *substandard English,* but, instead, to use this term for slang.

Home equity loan   Clearly more euphonious than the earthier second mortgage loan.

Home-protection weapon   A way of not saying gun.

Honor killing   Culturally approved practice in certain fundamentalist regions of the world in which fathers slaughter their daughters who have been raped.

Honorarium   The Latin word which appears to mollify recipients, typically academics, when they receive compensation that would doubtless be higher if it were simply called a payment.

Hook-ups   Since the 1990s, the phrase has meant a wide range of sexual encounters between casual acquaintances who have no plans or motivation to continue seeing one another. If charting romantic relationships statistically, hook-ups fall at the far tail of the bell-shaped curve.

Hot buildings   Commercial office structures offering wi-fi Internet access to lure prospective occupants.

Housekeeper   The term *cleaning lady* or *cleaning woman* is long gone from politically correct educational texts, replaced with this term.

Human intelligence collectors   This is the Pentagon's characterization for those who serve as interrogators. Whether the revised nomenclature has anything to do with modifications in conventionally accepted procedures in flushing information from those captured is an open question.

Human race   The human species made up of countless peoples that are classified into distinctive groups, which more properly might be termed the human races.

Human rights   The inalienable rights of every man and woman that cannot be denied by any government—to be protected from inhumane treatment and punishment, and to be allowed political beliefs and freedom, free speech, religious freedom and the right to fair and equitable treatment in the courts. The level of passionate concern about violations of these rights domestically and internationally is typically a reflection of the difference in the political position of those termed liberals or conservatives.

Hurry sickness   A malady afflicting Type A personalities.

I

I feel your pain   A new age expression of sympathy, not helped by Christina Aguilera rhyming it with "even in the rain."

I hear you   A term used primarily by politicians to indicate that they understand your statement or viewpoint, while avoiding any promise regarding anticipated action on the issue.

Idea whose time has come   A phrase used by political and or social activists, as well as Madison Avenue spin merchants, to identify a cause or product they hope you will endorse.

Ideologue   Someone guilty of clinging to principles in political discourse especially when the position espoused is judged to be contrary to mainstream convictions.

Illegal entrants   In 1942, wartime labor shortages resulted in the "Bracero Program," whereby temporary work visas allowed millions of Mexican laborers to be employed on Southwest US farms and ranches. Many stayed on with expired visas, and others arrived without visas and soon outnumbered the braceros three to one. As a result, federal officials returned one million-plus undocumented workers to Mexico in 1954 in an insensitively named program called "Operation Wetback," an action applauded by the media and politicians as necessary to the economic stability of the US. Sociologists today often use the term "undocumented immigrants" for these border crossers; *The Los Angeles Times* calls them illegal crossers, illegal immigrants, or undocumented immigrants. Former Homeland

Security Secretary Tom Ridge in December 2003 described them as "illegal immigrants" adding that the vast majority are not a threat to national security and should be given "some sort of legal status." The Tucson-based Arizona Daily Star, sympathetic to their plight, refers to them as "illegal entrants," and conservative Arizona Senator Jon Kyl and Scottsdale Congressman J.D. Hayworth often call them simply "illegals," while the National Council of La Raza refers to them as "undocumented immigrants." The legislative proposals often refer to the large population as "illegal entrants" and suggest they be recycled into a "guest worker" program.

Impact authentication devices The Bureau of Public Roads language for the oil drums placed along highway obstructions, a bureaucratic tour de force.

Immediate A Department of State cable classification meaning that the embassy communicators are to send it off to Washington—or elsewhere—as soon as possible, jumping the queue over lesser-designated cables. Once arrived, it is to be delivered immediately (during office hours) in Washington. There is a group of people in Washington who read incoming traffic after office hours and have the authority either to deal with it right away, or allow the message to wend its way to the addressees during business hours. The diplomatic community knows such a designation indicates an urgent policy matter, a death, or that the cable should be read before the Washington staff cut out early to beat the traffic, especially on Fridays. Immediate cables arriving at overseas posts on weekends are first read by a US marine if the cable arrives at night because he or she has to stay up all night anyway on guard duty. The marine, unless an old hand at this, will phone the responsible officer, wake that person up, be thanked for the information and told it can be dealt with on Monday. On Saturday, Sunday and holidays, cable traffic is read by a low-ranking "duty officer" who shows up for a few hours during the day. The officer sorts the cables into things that can be dealt with on Monday and those needing immediate attention, then phones the residence of those responsible for acting on the immediate cables. Much like the phone call to HQ from the radar crew at Pearl Harbor who spotted incoming blips on December 7, 1941, the responsible person almost always suggests the matter can be dealt with on Monday—now where is my tennis racquet?

Improper source dependence   Infinitely softer sounding than the harsher word for the same action—plagiarism.

In about an hour   Much like physicists' concept of an ever-expanding universe, this phrase—which always requires double or quadruple that time—is what it takes to replace a flat tire, change your oil, get a prescription, or the estimated time when a delayed telephone, cable or computer technician will arrive.

In-depth study   A term used in the media meaning a substantial discussion of an issue, often an entire segment of a half–hour program devoted to the issue, or, in newspaper parlance, a slow-news day requiring the insertion of an off-the-shelf filler, usually written by the editor's nephew.

In God we trust   The innocuous mention of God on coins that has been termed ceremonial deism, which has lost any religious significance. Some call the phrase religion fossilized into patriotism. While the reference to a deity holds religious meaning for some, atheists and many others loathe the use of this language inscribed and prescribed on the coins of the realm.

In one way or another   This is the term modifying compliance requirements used by Bush II's Secretary of Defense Donald Rumsfeld before the Senate Armed Services Committee in May 2004 discussing the mistreatment of Iraqi prisoners by members of the US armed forces in violation of law—both US and international. Rumsfeld observed that the US guards' instructions are to adhere to the Geneva Conventions. The Geneva Conventions apply to all of the individuals there in one way or another. Previously, in an April 7, 2003, Department of Defense release, W. Hays Parks, special assistant to the Judge Advocate General for the Army, complained that the "Iraqi regime is not complying with the Geneva Conventions." Maybe they were, in one way or another. *See also Appropriate, Detainees, Enemy Combatants, Extraordinary Rendition, Interrogation, O.G.A., Physical Pressure, Softening up, Stress Positions*

In touch with your feelings   What we used to call emotional.

Inappropriate words   A term used by the Office of Foreign Assets Control (OFAC) of the Treasury Department to criminalize the editing of an article, book or even a poem for eventual publication if the written material was provided by a citizen of an embargoed country such as Cuba. Prior to this Bush II Administration ruling, such writings were protected by the First Amendment of the US Constitution. But the OFAC sees the "reordering of paragraphs or sentences, correction of syntax, grammar and replacement of inappropriate words" or the addition of an illustration makes those editorial functions a "service" you are providing to a citizen of an embargoed country, and thus punishable by up to 10 years in prison. In December of 2004, the Treasury Department issued a revised ruling allowing those manuscripts to be edited and published in the US, but only if the US publisher does not have to deal with an official foreign government representative.

Incompetent   A favored political descriptor, used in 2004 by House Minority Leader Nancy Pelosi, to describe the kind of leader she views President Bush to be, and by conservative talking-head Rush Limbaugh in a reference to Senator Kerry's leadership in Vietnam. While Pelosi has first hand knowledge of the Bush leadership, Limbaugh has never served in Vietnam.

Incontinent ordnance   A Department of Defense term for artillery shells bursting on civilians.

Incubator space   The provision of rental areas for start-up companies on or adjacent to university campuses. The objective is to help foster new companies, frequently high tech firms, by making available low-rent space, inexpensive business services and proximity to faculty members for consultation or joint efforts.

Indefinite idling   You don't have to pay severance pay, reasoned the management of a steel company closing a plant and thus terminating employment of its workers, if you are not firing them, just allowing them to stay home, using this term to describe that process.

Independent Counsel   An attorney appointed by the Attorney General of the US, funded under legislation of the US Congress. While this statute was in force—it expired in 1999—it poured massive amounts of funds into teams of investigators. With few limitations, these operatives scrutinized activities of high-ranking Administration officials and the President, looking for misconduct. These investigations included the Nixon Administration's Watergate, Reagan's Iran-Contra and Clinton's relationship with former White House intern Monica Lewinsky.

Infielder   As in first base infielder. Try saying that rapidly during a double play. In any case, the term baseman is banned by at least one educational textbook and we are told to use this term instead.

Infomercials   The term characterizing TV programs presumably intended to entertain viewers but, using the format of a news documentary, hawk goods and services and huckster all kinds of consumer products that are completely devoid of any other content.

Information Resource Center   The term for library, particularly in schools, but also in other contexts where high flown verbiage holds appeal.

Information society   While it is true that the Web allows access to massive collections of printed matter in electronic form, cognition requires the investment in time to receive and ponder. American television programming presents information as audio side-bars to the visuals, and discussions on a topic are reduced to talking heads volleying opposing sound-bites. Traditional information acquisition, whereby a subject is explored from thesis to supporting argument, has disappeared. Now there is no time to access, no time to consider, no time to digest information into knowledge. Using the wonders of the Web just for shopping doesn't count, which is akin to being well read by driving by your bookstore on the freeway.

Information specialist   The person otherwise known as a librarian.

Inner city   Also called blighted neighborhoods, ghetto or slum.

Insourcing   A reference to keeping the tasks and responsibilities within an organization, or within the same country, as opposed to outsourcing. Outsourcing usually wins the economic arguments, but governments and pundits are keen to buck economic realities with political concerns about lost jobs, lost markets and lost technology. The drive to obtain the latest technology trumps containment efforts, no matter how draconian the punishment, from the loss of silk weaving technology to Anatolia in the 5th century, British cotton-spinning technology to the Yanks after the American Revolution, and American atomic weaponry to America's allies and enemies alike after World War II.

Intellectual   The textbook publisher Houghton Mifflin suggests to its writers that this is preferable (and somehow a synonym) to *bookworm*.

Intellectually stunted   What once was termed a stupid person.

Intelligence specialist   A person hired to gather and assess information about another country or industry, usually with training in the culture and language of that locale; in the military, this person is trained to assess military capabilities, in industry to assess technological and scientific advances of the competition; also known as a secret agent or spy.

Intelligent design   What used to be known as "creationism." The belief that the world around us is too complex to have simply bumbled into being; instead it required a sensate being to design it. This belief is in opposition to over 100 years of research in genetics, the fossil record and myriad disciplines making use of the scientific method. Einstein, asked about those who rejected the scientific evidence of the origin of life on earth, suggested kindly in a sort of oral relativity phrase, that "it is a belief, if you believe it." Since about half of Americans reject Darwin's theory of evolution, there is increasing pressure on legislatures, school boards and publishers to delimit the teaching of evolution.

Intercommunal warfare   A term used by the Turkish government in reference to Ottoman Turkey's mass killing, forced deportation, starvation, rape and exposure to typhus and other diseases that wiped out a quarter of the Armenians living in Turkey during World War I.

Interface   While at one time it simply meant a device that communicates with something else, it has evolved to mean the way a computer interacts with a human. Unfortunately, the term has been taken up by human-potential trainers to mean simply the interaction between people.

Interfacing electronically   Making telephone calls.

International medical graduate   The politically correct term referencing what was once known as a foreign medical graduate, or a physician educated outside the United States.

Interrogation   In all too many instances in Afghanistan and Iraq, this term meant that US forces elicited information from a prisoner by torture.

Intrapreneurship   The alternative to the classic style of the top-down, corporate management-run organization. This model reasons that people in a company should compete just as strongly against each other as they do against other corporations. By fostering strong internal competition among independent internal units the weaker ones will either improve or fail to survive. Enron was a testing ground for this strategy.

Intrusion-free shopping environment   The term used by a spokesperson for New Jersey shopping malls that had attempted to ban the distribution of leaflets to shoppers. The New Jersey Supreme Court ruled that leafleting must be permitted, allowing mall visitors both to shop and consider issues that might be equal in importance to finding the next bargain.

Inventory leakage   In the mercantile world, this means shoplifted items.

Irrefutable evidence   In the Bush II Administration, it means that it would be impolite or impolitic to refute the claim. This was, after all, the term that launched a thousand warheads and burnt the topless towers of Baghdad. In 2004 we discovered that the 2002-2003 use of this term by Vice President Dick Cheney and Condoleezza Rice, referencing a large pile of aluminum tubes in the possession of Saddam Hussein, were not nuclear centrifuges, as we were told. In October 2004 we learned that senior American nuclear scientists knew—and told the Administration—that the tubes were too narrow, too thick and too shiny (meaning coated) to be part of Iraq's nuclear plans.

Isn't that special   A complimentary term that avoids giving any real feedback as to what you are in fact thinking, good or—just as likely—bad.

Issues   For example, magazine editors these days refer to having issues with rock stars who are not forthcoming with their personal lives, who interview poorly. Read personal problems or "differences."

J

Jack-booted government thugs   In one of its numerous fund-raising appeals, the National Rifle Association coined the term to characterize the agents of the government whom they charge with the harassment, intimidation and even murder of law-abiding citizens who own guns.

Japander   The word for western entertainment luminaries like Mel Gibson and Brad Pitt who have succumbed to the Nipponese yen for Western performers by appearing in Japanese advertising.

Jefferson muzzles   The apt description for the awards to individuals and organizations who have taken a position that flagrantly blocks freedom of speech and public expression. It has been sponsored annually since 1992 by the Thomas Jefferson Center for the Protection of Free Expression of Charlottesville, Virginia. Among the celebrated recipients is former Attorney General John Ashcroft for promotion of the USA Patriot Act and the other measures in the aftermath of 9/11.

Joe six-pack   The negative stereotyping of males at the low end of the economic scale.

Junk science   A term meaning that the scientific evidence is wrong, given that it disagrees with the political agendas of the far right and corporate lobbyists.

Just war   The phrase used by self-defined patriots for any armed conflict in which their nation is engaged.

Juvenile delinquent   Underage criminal.

Kickback   A bribe, illegal in the US but often the only way of getting a government contract in many countries around the world.

Killing box   A military term, as well as a popular book and music group. Its military use references an electronic grid or map coordinates to search and target installations or persons, often with high tech weaponry.

Kinder, gentler conservatism   A meaningless phrase Bush I's speechwriters used, hinting that his policies would be more compassionate than those of President Reagan.

Kitsch   Description for tasteless and pretentious art, literature or performance in spite of or perhaps because of its widespread popular appeal.

Knowledge management   A term first appearing in 1986, with increased popularity after 1996. Professor T.D. Wilson, an information scientist, who ought to know what it means, suggests the term "is an umbrella term for a variety of organizational activities, none of which are concerned with the management of knowledge...(but is used to describe) the management of work practices, in the expectation that changes in such communication practice will enable information sharing." If the concept remains unclear, consider that librarians in the World Bank working as knowledge managers get paid more. What they do there is encourage information exchange among department members, provide access to information and experts via indices and intranets, and create newsgroups for staff members; in short, work as a utility outfielder for their department's information needs.

Known knowns   A felicitous February 12, 2002, phrase of Bush II's Secretary of Defense, Donald Rumsfeld, explaining to the press, "as we know, there are known knowns, these are things we know we know. We also know there are known unknowns. That is to say there are some things we do not know. But there are also unknown unknowns, the ones we don't know we don't know."

L

L-word Besides the television drama by that name, referencing lesbians, the more common understanding is that the L-word stands for liberalism. The concept of a liberal politician is so threatening to nativist Americans that Bush I used it in an attempt to demonize the very concept when running against then Governor Clinton. The cute abbreviation allows the speaker to suggest the term is too naughty to be spoken in polite company. Like father like son: Bush II, in his reelection debates with Senator John Kerry, pointing to the National Journal as his source, stated that Kerry was the "most liberal" member of the US Senate in 2003, prompting a new generation of headline writers to use this term.

Lad lit The name of the genre of new books streaming forth from publishers aimed at younger male readers. Similar targeted publishing includes chick lit, with its Bridget Jones-type books about the lives, times and foibles of thirty-something women. *See also Chick lit.*

Language arts Don't try to find the word *English* in the department headings of schools these days; all too often the word has been modernized to you-know-what. Still holding fast to the English Department title are traditional establishments such as Princeton High School, in Princeton, New Jersey. John McPhee, a student there in the 1950s, has acknowledged his debt to the English teachers who contributed, of course, to the making of a language artist.

Latchkey child An estimated 65 percent of young school-age children in America return to an empty home because their parents are working. The children are expected to take care of themselves, usually with a flickering television for company.

Law and order   Expression favored by the right when stirring "crime in the street" into political stewpots.

Lawfare   Making use of legal stratagems and transnational law in pursuit of your strategic aims.

Lay a guilt trip on   Today's term for a direct or implied accusation.

Leader   Remember when you return from the Brazilian jungles to describe your meeting with the tribal leader, not the headman, which is no longer politically correct.

Lean initiative   Corporate buzzwords used when management introduces new cost-reduction measures.

Learning facilitation   Another Latinate creation from the contemporary education lexicon for the simple and understandable word—teaching.

Learning resource center   Like the Information Resources Center, this term is popularly called the library.

Least best   Complicated way to express worst.

Leaving to pursue other options   In a time when no one gets fired from a job anymore this phrase, or "leaving to spend more time with the family," have become the preferred surrogates.

Left-brained *see* **Right-brained**

Legacy preference   The boost which many colleges and universities give in admission selection to applicants who are children or family members of alumni. The practice of favoring sons and daughters of alumni is most often found in elite schools. A 2004 Democratic Presidential contender, Senator John Edwards, dismissed it as "a birthright cult of 18th century British aristocracy, not 21st century American democracy."

Lesbo drama   Unambiguous representation of lesbians and lesbian behavior as a distinct element in popular culture in stage and television performance.

Liberal   A word transformed into almost an expletive by the propagandists of the far right, implying such traits as elitism, political correctness, immorality and socialist thinking to characterize the tenets of liberals. For those on the left the word conveys a belief in the dynamism and creativity of democratic capitalism incorporating a strong active government to protect societal interests and ensuring real opportunities and decent living standards for everyone. Or, in their view, moderate or centrist views.

Liberal guilt   Coined by conservatives to ridicule what they view as bleeding heart inclinations toward society's poor and marginal people.

Liberate   An alternative for the more belligerent sounding word, invade. Its roots can be traced to World War II, when it was first employed by the Allied Military Force to characterize the D-Day assault into France.

Lifelong learning   This usually means either job training or adults, particularly seniors, taking courses.

Like so five minutes ago   A teen term for a once popular trend that is now embarrassingly passé, for example, trendy teens in Hong Kong and Singapore have forgone the "dance dance revolution" to congregate in shopping malls to the newest craze, "parapara dancing."

Likely   When intelligence analysts use this term, it means they believe there is a 60-70 percent chance the hypothesis is correct.

Limited war   This can be any form of armed conflict short of nuclear cataclysm. It may be controlled and localized but it is still devastating to the people of the nations involved.

Limousine liberal   Characterized by the right as the whimsical luxury of the very rich who are said to espouse such tenets as modest life style, equal housing, equal pay and environmental improvement while they are enjoying and flaunting their very flamboyant personal manner of living. The term was coined by Mario Procaccino who lost the mayoralty race in New York in 1969 to John Lindsay, portraying him as a well-off reformer who advocated integration of public schools while sending his own children to private ones.

Link popularity   An online marketing term that measures the prominence of a site by two scales: the quantity of sites linking to it, and the quality of those sites. In a sort of assessment–by–the–company–you–keep, the linking to the site from a major directory carries more weight than your cousin's Web site on his beer bottle collection. This was one of Google's innovations from day one.

Lipstick indicator   The sales graphing of moderately priced consumer luxury goods, such as women's beauty products, bracketing downturns in the economy.

Liquidity crisis   What some business people call a cash flow problem or the inability to pay current debts due for payment because of a shortage of ready funds. Liquid implies money available for use, unlike assets such as plant, equipment, unsold inventory and receivables due but not yet on hand. Sometimes, however, the term is simply a surrogate for what is an imminent bankruptcy.

LOAEL   An acronym for Lowest Observed Adverse Effect Level. A stressor, we are told, that is akin to that chap seated behind you at the airport whose loud conversation finally sparks you to jump up and ask him to lower his voice. In terms of health and ecological risk, the flash point or lowest tested dose with which a physical, biological or chemical stressor has been found to trigger harmful health effects on animals or people is the LOAEL. If some cruel god were to surround you in the same airport with hundreds of louts babbling on their cell phones and you simply did not react, it would be similar to the NOAEL factor, which stands for No Observed Adverse Effects Level. That means that the stressor, even with the highest count of cell phone babblers we could round up, or the highest level of chemical stressors we tried in a toxicity test, were found to not cause harmful effects. Those terms are bandied about in the Bush II's "sound science" group and its new tool, the "Data Quality Act." (See separate entry) Scientists have proven that a leading US farm weed killer disrupts the hormones of exposed wildlife. That evidence was enough to get the weed killer banned in Europe. Farmers still use it in the US because scientists don't know for certain if it is messing with *your* insides. The "sound science" administrators making use of their Data Quality Act means that if it looks like a duck, and sounds like a duck, we can call it a duck only after examining an unprecedented level of scientific certainty involving massive testing and mountains of data. Only then, can regulations be issued to protect you and me.

Lobbyists   Those who engage for pay in carrying out activities of every imaginable or unimaginable kind, directed toward influencing legislative or administrative actions at the federal, state, county or local level, by communicating their views to publicly elected or appointed officials in order to sway them toward enacting or sometimes rejecting statutes or regulations, consistent with the interests of those who employ the lobbyist.

Log Cabin Republicans   The designation of those who identify themselves as homosexual male and female Republicans and support such values as individual responsibility, and who consequently reject governmental intrusion into the personal and private lives of the citizenry.

Log rolling   A term for those enthusing blurbs found on book jackets which are often, alas, a quid pro quo back scratch whereby authors represented by the same agent or same publisher do the needful. The practice is not unknown in Amazon's "customer reviews," with friends and family offering their anonymous praises to Uncle George's book.

Low-hanging fruit   A term implying an easily obtained goal, easy pickings. Used in the research community to describe projects that are not looking for complex, overarching principles, but easy targets of investigation.

Low-income   What the Census Bureau used to term poverty, as in "below the poverty level." The term, long ago, was 'the poor.'

Low-maintenance   In real estate, the term is linked with yard, meaning the area is paved, except in the Southwest, where it refers to a crushed rock surface. In either case, it is truly trouble free—no worries about Bermuda grass or grub infestations. In sociology, the term refers to undemanding relationships, such as with your dog.

Loyal opposition   The political stance of members of the opposing party who serve as spear carriers, lining up to stand behind and lend their support and their votes to the other side.

Ludology   This is a new branch of academic study—how the fantastically popular form of computer games has made addicts of half the Americans over the age of six. The discipline looks at human behavior and social interactions related to this software. This term for game studies comes from the Latin word for games and has nothing to do with the Luddites, who are reportedly spinning in their graves.

Lulu   A real estate and urban planner's term for the opposite of "'desirable neighborhoods," that being land surrounding power stations, penal institutions and the like that results in local, unwanted land.

Machers　The appellation for those wheeler-dealers in business and government who are able to get things done effortlessly. The word originated as a Yiddish expression, derived from the German verb machen, to make, to do, to provide.

Magalog　New form of publication—a hybrid of a magazine and a catalog. This is cutting edge updating of the conventional sales catalog, connecting topical articles on style, fashion and cool trends in modern living with displays of merchandise to entice readers to buy, buy, buy.

Magical thinking　The belief that your views, thoughts and activities somehow impact the outcome of events, counter to the laws of physics and logic. This phenomenon of hoped-for, but unrealistic results to an action are common in fairy tales, young children's dreams and Bush II's plans for "cutting the deficit in half," finding "weapons of mass destruction," stem-cell research, global warming, and other areas, whereby what is hoped for from "sound science" has proven to be as valid as Lysenko's politically motivated genetic theories.

Mainstream media　The term for TV, radio and press communication forums through which the news of the day reaches the largest number of American readers and viewers. That definition of the term is uncontested. The controversy revolves about whether these so called mainstream media reflect a bias in their reporting content and style. Naturally the right wing sees a problem with liberal bias among most of the newspaper and TV fare and the liberals claim exactly the reverse. Maybe there is some truth in the reason of both sides; but the most obvious bias grows out of the profit motives of the mainstream media with their ubiquitous coverage of scandals, sensational stories, sex and violence and their perception that their talking heads can really explain difficult issues with their brief sound bites.

Maintenance person   This is what, in the olden days, we called a handyman.

Making a difference   A term often heard at commencement exercises and memorial services suggesting that certain activities of the graduate or deceased are morally charged, having a positive impact on others. It is not applied, no matter what the seeming logic, in reference to those who have caused cataclysmic damage to others, such as mass murderers or industrial polluters. The term is a favorite for recruiting nurses, teachers and others to enter the lower paying professions.

Making things perfectly clear   Ever since President Richard Nixon, it has evolved into a phrase employed by politicians to prefix a blatant obfuscation or outright lie.

Malcontents   A term used in May 2004 by Dan Senor, a Senior Adviser to L. Paul Bremer III, former Administrator of the Coalition Provisional Authority, the occupation government in Iraq, in the statement, "Baathists, Saddamists, terrorists and other malcontents are trying to derail the sovereignty process by engaging in violence." This useful epithet has been employed since malcontenti in Florence were burned at the stake in picturesque piazzas. Their crime was, as the dictionary says, "actively discontented, and indisposed to acquiesce in the existing administration of affairs."

Managed care   A system of health care delivery usually organized by insurance carriers but also by employers and hospitals. Payment is on a fixed basis and is intended to provide participants with the care they require by keeping costs down and improving quality. Only those who can afford to pay the costs through their employment or insurance plans are covered, leaving out over 40 million Americans. The costs of managed care are constantly rising and HMOs (Health Maintenance Organizations) use from 15 percent to 33 percent of every premium dollar to cover profits and overhead.

Managed news   This is information, imparted by those responsible for sharing it with the media, which is purported to be real news but is instead manipulated and contrived, seldom conveying any content serving the public interest.

Management consultant   An individual or firm specializing in applying expertise in resolving business and government problems. The field has burgeoned since the 1980s with many large firms regularly engaging their services for specific projects and overseeing major internal reorganizations for them. Sometimes, however, this is a an honorific title used in industry for farming out no longer wanted senior staff.

Management guru   An authority in the business world celebrated for writing, advising, or preaching concepts and theories which frequently question conventional wisdom or practice. Many are academics in business schools or economics departments who sometimes propagate fashionable trends or fads. Gurus achieve their lofty status through catchy and artful remarks and sometimes they have led successful giant companies. What they have in common are their monumental lecture fees and their desire that their books become bestsellers.

Managing the blood supply   Concentrating on monitoring the work force in a company to ensure that there is no deviation in strategy, or diminution of the quality of performance and flow of innovative ideas all through the organization.

Manufactured home   An upscale and, for once, correct term for what most call a mobile home. These housing units built in factories, in fact have—hidden from view—trailer frames, axels, wheels and tow hitches, but are hauled to their final destination by a tractor trailer. Once planted on a plat—often rented space—in a trailer park (mobile home park), they almost always stay put, unless moved about, as seen on newscasts, by tornadoes and hurricanes.

Manufacturing czar   George W. Bush's September 1, 2003, Labor Day speech at a factory training center in Ohio, sporting a just-folks baseball cap and open-collared shirt, spoke of creating a high-level government post in the Commerce Department to nurture the "manufacturing sector." This new position, nicknamed a "manufacturing czar" by business and the media, had, unfortunately, the markings of a hollow gesture. At least Presidential candidate Senator John Kerry thought so, observing, "it took six months for the Bush Administration to actually announce a candidate," and noted during that time, "the nation lost more than 96,000 jobs." When it became known that the candidate finally selected, Tony Raimondo, head of the Behlen Manufacturing Company, had laid off a sixth of his work force in 2002 and was opening a new plant in China, the nomination fizzled. A March 13, 2004, New York Times editorial noted, "the new post seemed a ploy to paper over the fact that Mr. Bush's deficit-feeding tax cuts for the wealthy have failed to create the millions of new jobs he promised." The same editorial noted, "the unemployment challenge deserves more considered remedies than the appointment of a man who could never pass political muster to a job that never seemed serious." On November 21, 2004, a manufacturing czar was appointed, the honorable Albert Frink, Jr., a California luxury carpet maker who was shoved into a former assistant secretary for trade's office in the Department of Commerce.

Market timing   The practice by which some investors take advantage of the fact that mutual fund prices do not change during the day the way stock prices do. Instead they are set once at 4 p.m., New York Stock Exchange (NYSE) time. Buyers before 4 p.m. purchase their shares at that day's price and buyers after 4 p.m. get the next day's price. But markets overseas close at different times. For example, the Tokyo Stock Exchange closes at 2 a.m., long before the 4 p.m. NYSE time closing. If some event takes place in the US markets before 4 p.m. that is likely to increase overseas market price values the next day, market timers buy shares in mutual funds made up of international or foreign stocks at the current price, which is cheaper than the likely price in the US the following day. Then they sell the shares the next day at a profit. And all this is legal. "Late trading," however, is illegal. This happens when investment groups conspire with mutual fund managements to buy shares in a fund after 4 p.m. while still paying that day's price. Thus, if important news breaks after 4 p.m. that is likely to raise the market and therefore the funds' value the next day, they buy the funds' shares and sell them for a virtually guaranteed profit the next day. It's illegal because this is somewhat like being able to bet on a horse race after it has run. Perhaps it is not surprising that a number of mutual fund managements and brokerage houses have been implicated in conducting such practices.

Marketroid   A derisive term used by computer software engineers referring to a member of their organization's marketing department. Software engineers will assure you that these individuals make their lives difficult by promising the customer features that cannot possibly be included or that were simply not planned for inclusion, and speak in a separate, therefore inferior, jargon to their own.

Massage   To enhance not only your body tone, but also corporate or government reports; an enhancement or overstatement of the case, without the bother of facts to back it up.

The Match   Shorthand for the National Resident Matching Program. This is a system begun in 1952 to bring order to what had been a chaotic process through which medical school graduates and hospitals connect. It has grown into a computerized program that allows the medical graduates to interview with a number of residency programs and then to list their preferences. Hospitals likewise list their preferences and the system then plays matchmaker. In 2002, The Match filled 18,447 residency positions of the 20,602 offered. But is the clearinghouse system, in effect, collusion between hospitals to prevent residents from negotiating higher pay, shorter hours and better working conditions? Recent federal legislation has had the effect of blocking any litigation for the claims against that practice by the medical graduates. But difficulties remain and can be expected to give rise to further legal challenges by disgruntled residents.

MATRIX (Multi-State Anti-Terrorism Information Exchange)   Federally funded crime and terrorism database intended to make possible the quick access to billions of pieces of information. It is being promoted as an ultra-efficient way for investigators to get information about suspects that otherwise would have to be obtained from countless sources. The number of states participating is growing with important jurisdictions like Connecticut, Florida, Michigan, New York, Ohio and Pennsylvania enrolled. Privacy advocates complain that the system offers too much access to the private and personal details of millions of people.

Matrix organization   This term refers to a form of company management that attempts to unclog bureaucratic arteries by drawing upon the expertise and skills of staff from any sector of the organization to address a particular issue. Some of America's major companies, as well as hospitals and think tanks, make use of this model. Management gurus often love this design, claiming you get a clearer picture of corporate opportunities, you can avoid institutional potholes, and you can move faster than the competition to identify innovative solutions. But because you work for two people, your functional boss and your product boss, both yank you in different directions, and if one of the two is slow to move to the next step in the project the team twists in the wind with no real supervisor there to cut you down. Since most organizations have lost whole sectors of expertise in downsizing, you are also expected to cover for all those retired specialists, now sipping pina coladas in their time-shares in Majorca.

Mature   An economic term for a down-sliding economy, a media term usually involving explicit sex scenes, and an advertising term suggesting their products are just what an old, retired person needs.

Maximizer see **Satisficer**

McMansions   The flip side of the coin from the itsy-bitsy, ticky-tacky housing of post-World War II. Today's constructions are enormously oversized private homes with vast entryways, bathrooms resembling dry-docks and all squeezed onto a tiny lot a poof-ball's throw from the neighbors.

McProfiling   In a version of you-are-what-you-drive, fast-food restaurants now have the option of using a system called "Hyperactive

Bob" whose cameras monitor vehicles entering their parking lot. The system correlates vehicles with that model's typical order. Thus, before you enter the restaurant, the preparation has begun. The system apparently cuts waste and preparation time.

Meaningful dialogue   A press officer's term masking the fact that nothing was accomplished during the meeting.

Media bias   It used to be that this meant solely partiality or partisanship rather than accuracy and objectivity, thereby reflecting deliberate efforts to distort events. In recent years media bias is also seen to stem from the conscious or unconscious predilections which slant perception of news so that objectivity is but a delusion. Critics of the left view the newspaper and broadcast media as overly tilted toward the right while the rightists naturally see journalists and commentators as heavily supporting the leftist agenda. Of course, the right wing of American politics, whether true victims of media bias or merely victims of their own paranoia, have long felt vilified by popular culture, which they charge depicts them as heartless creatures without any human compassion.

Media center   Still another description for what used to be called a library.

Media specialist   A person whose role is typically identified as librarian.

Medicine of desires   This is a term used by Pope John Paul II in 2002 for such things as plastic surgery and in vitro fertilization, medical practices that he viewed as "contrary to the moral good," serving the pursuit of pleasure rather than the eradication of poverty, and driven by "the overriding financial interests" of biomedical and pharmaceutical research.

Meetling   The staff member who appears to do nothing other than arrange for and participate in endless conferences and meetings.

Meet-up   A local political rally typically held at someone's home, organized via email or a Web site and popularized in the 2004 Presidential election.

Member of Congress   Major textbook publishers ask you to use this term, or alternatively Representative, rather than Congressman.

MEMCON   A State Department acronym for memorandum of conversation, whereby a US diplomat drafts a report on a conversation with certain foreign contacts. An often ignored requirement in Cold War days when working in the Soviet Union and its satellites, since compliance would have required staffers to spend half their time drafting such reports. However, selected "official conversations" did result in such a document. In embassies, the officers usually turn in these reports to the embassy security officer, who forwards them to Washington, either by "pouch" or electronically: "cable" in dip-speak.

Meme   A theme, concept or conceit in dress, behavior or speech. The idea is that these are cell-like cultural building blocks, be it a Nike "swoosh" or an advertising jingle or phrase such as "whatever," that have become absorbed components of our culture. Their pervasiveness is facilitated by the news media and the Internet.

Merit system   The promotion scheme designed to advance employees in government and business based upon performance rather than seniority or connections. For many in the liberal camp such a system is seen as the means of neglecting the enforcement of equal rights and affirmative action measures. Others see meritorious performance as the only fair means of promotion even if minority group members may be at a disadvantage. The up or out merit system used in the US military and the foreign service has led to inflated walk-on-water evaluations for favored individuals, but does recognize and promote talented people who have acquired requisite skills and training.

Mess   What you call the dog and cat excrement on your lawn. What you call the dog or cat is another matter.

Meth orphans   Kids who find themselves out in the cold when their parents are imprisoned or die from an overdose of methamphetamines.

Metoobees   Those participants in online conferences and chat rooms who are incapable of any response but "I agree," "me too" and "ditto."

Metrodox   Jewish orthodox urban dwellers who strive for a balance between their religious beliefs and trendy young life styles.

Metrosexual   Urban heterosexual modern man preoccupied with clothing, money and style, even to the point of following the personal grooming rituals conventionally considered female, such as waxing, exfoliating and other beauty treatments.

Micetronauts   The Mars Society has developed a proposal for dispatching mice into space, in order to learn the effects of their living and procreating under conditions of reduced gravity, and to gain intelligence which might be useful in the planning for eventually sending human space travelers to Mars.

Middle America   The millions of Americans with limited savings and uncertain prospects for the future, whose values and political outlook are influenced by the changing tide of economic, social and religious trends.

Midlife crisis   The notion that men and women between the ages of 40 and 60 live a life of constant stress and turmoil has been exposed by researchers to be a myth. The truth is that specialists continue to identify more young people suffering from depression and stress-related illnesses than those of more mature years.

Middle Class Bill of Rights   This refers to a particular piece of legislation introduced by President Bill Clinton in 1994, which has all but vanished from the political radar screen. It proposed an altruistic plan modeled somewhat after the post-World War II GI Bill, but this time intended to help working people gain the education and skills needed in order to provide them a more equitable base in the new American economy.

Middle East road map   Ostensibly this is the projected plan for peace in the Middle East, which, according to the State Department, "is performance-based and goal driven with clear phases, timetables, target dates and benchmarks aiming at progress through reciprocal steps by the two parties in the political, security, economic, humanitarian and institution-building fields, under the auspices of the Quartet (US, European Union, United Nations and Russia)." The destination is a final and comprehensive settlement of the Israel-Palestinian conflict by 2005. It was enunciated in 2003 by President George W. Bush. But the vehicle traversing the road broke down before the journey was begun or perhaps the White House simply lost the map.

Mild irregularity　Advertising copy for the last unmentionable on TV, constipation.

Military advisers　Soldiers who are ostensibly sent to educate and train the fighting force of a foreign land rather than engaging in combat themselves. The terminology dates back to the Spanish Civil War and was rekindled with American involvement with the South Vietnamese military in the 1950s when the first US troops were dispatched there, and again, in the 1970s when American troopers went to Angola to counter a Cuban military presence there.

Military industrial complex　The famous cautionary remarks by President Dwight D. Eisenhower about the perils of cozy relationships between the Pentagon and corporate behemoths soliciting military business were made in a landmark 1961 speech, three days before he left office. President Eisenhower warned, "[i]n the councils of government, we must guard against the acquisition of unwarranted influence, whether sought or unsought, by the military-industrial complex. The potential for the disastrous rise of misplaced power exists and will persist. We must never let the weight of this combination endanger our liberties or democratic processes. We should take nothing for granted. Only an alert and knowledgeable citizenry can compel the proper meshing of the huge industrial and military machinery of defense with our peaceful methods and goals, so that security and liberty may prosper together."

Military procurement　The system under which the federal government buys weaponry and purchases services from private corporations. When Uncle Sam goes shopping, his shopping cart often is pushed by former military personnel and another former member of the armed forces is at the shop's cash register. This non-coincidence has contributed to periodic public outrages. Scandals have been cropping up since Senator Harry Truman started investigating defense plants in the 1940s and have not diminished since. Fraudulent contracts usually are found to relate to the political motivations in the choice of contractors, what the contractors said they would do vis-à-vis what they actually did, and who evaluates the results of contracts. Too often the involved parties are in the same bed, without the benefit of bundling boards.

Militia   Once this term described a group of citizens charged to perform military duties to protect the security of the state. In recent history it has come to mean small and, (outside the US) often large armed collectives committed to political and religious beliefs and dedicated to the use of arms to assault the authority structure.

Millennium Challenge Account   A new approach by the George W. Bush Administration intended to fundamentally overhaul those American programs that assist developing nations by creating competition among recipient countries to demonstrate their worthiness to receive assistance. Criteria that the administrative board overseeing the effort plans to follow in evaluating prospective recipient countries include per capita income levels below a specified point and demonstrated respect for civil liberties.

Mindshare   Media-speak for what used to be called public perception.

Minimize   Not a government policy making light of a problem, but a State Department term you must add to a cable going to an overseas embassy to acknowledge you know there is only token staff on hand to read it. Otherwise, embassies great and small are deluged daily with what one undiplomatic diplomat termed "mountains of crap." Promotion lists, the most read cables in any diplomatic outpost, are never minimized. Tiny outposts, however, qualify for a SEP (Special Embassy Program) whereby diplomatic and consular posts such as "AMEMBASSY DUSHABE" receive a reduced traffic load of cables and are exempted from many of the reporting requirements of the more substantial posts.

Misery index   An economic term that has nothing to do with how much you owe on your credit cards, but a quick test of a country's fiscal well being. You simply add the country's annual inflation rate to the unemployment rate to obtain this figure.

Mission accomplished   The somewhat premature victory remarks in May 2003 and the celebratory banner festooned on the aircraft carrier, the USS Lincoln, onto which George W. Bush, in military garb, landed Rambo-style in a Navy plane to herald the end of the Iraq war. He later pretended, not quite accurately, that the idea of the banner behind him was the Navy's idea rather than the Administration's.

Mission creep   A military term now used by the world at large for a change from an organization's original methods and goals, enlarging upon the original purpose, or becoming more diffuse, less focused, or skewing their activities away from the original direction. Example: when law enforcement agencies use the new laws intended to punish terrorists to crack down on currency smugglers and drug dealers.

Misspeak   The explanation proffered by politicians high and low for the bloopers occasioned by their recorded lapses of good sense in making impolite, offensive or absurd remarks.

Mistakes were made   Use of the passive form is a favorite of high government officials when seeking to dodge accountability and responsibility for their actions or the deeds of their subordinates.

Mobile home community   Also known as a trailer park.

Mobility challenged   The non-ambulatory who require a wheelchair for movement.

Mobility pool   If you look around at others in this pool, you will find you all have one thing in common—your company has just fired you.

Model   Here we are referring to a man or woman posing for advertising copy, not a facsimile. At least one educational publisher asks its writers to use this term when referring to someone gracing the covers of popular magazines rather than cover girl.

Moderate   The political position of those occupying the middle ground between liberal and conservative stands without holding fast to a deeply entrenched view. The definition of who is a moderate and who is not is in the eye of the beholder. The term is an equal opportunity designation used by the media and politicians themselves to characterize both Democrats and Republicans.

Moderator   In not-so-ancient sexist times, what was called a chairman, later shortened to chair.

Modern Republican   A term used by Dwight Eisenhower's speechwriters to distinguish him from the other candidates. It was never defined, and anyway, never caught on.

Modernized translation The term used by the Tyndale House publishers to herald their new version of the Bible, which, to meet present demographics, is pitched at the sixth grade reading level.

Mom lit To the burgeoning genre of books targeted at and penned by specific cultural sub-groups is this new outpouring of work focused on the life and times of young mothers. Much of it is fueled by the travails and anger of this new generation of women who have to cope with the requirements, pressures and contradictions of work (inside and outside the home), kids and husbands.

Mompreneurs Corporate female dropouts who have forsaken the business fast track to remain at home where they juggle their responsibilities as mothers with the launching of new enterprises, often using the Internet and eBay as their preferred route to profitability.

Mongo The word used for garbage which is salvaged by collectors from trash piles or discards found on the streets, whether or not it is useful, wearable or even describable, so long as it has some kind of appeal to the scrounger.

Monoculturism Denotes the way modern day advanced commercial media, for better or worse, propels a kind of universal cloning of common tastes, attitudes and consumer propensities among Americans and, by its ubiquitous globalization initiatives, among the peoples of other societies as well.

MOPs Millionaires on paper whose fortunes are in their company stock options. They are sometimes known as optionaires.

Moral hazard The term used by insurance companies for the problem that the insured may take greater risks than the non-insured since they know they are protected. Thus, the insurance company ends up paying out more claims than projected. This could explain the mind set of those people driving their RVs down mountain trails at high speed.

Mortality rate The death toll is the actual meaning.

Motion discomfort Cruise-speak for airsick or seasick. Starting a collection of motion discomfort bags? Look in eBay under the more informal "barf bags."

Mouse potato　　While the couch potato lies inert amidst shards of lost Fritos, shadows of a TV screen flickering across the body, the mouse potato's active fingers, at least, are eternally typing messages on a computer keyboard, chatting with fellow surfers.

Mousetrapping　　Akin to B'rer Fox's entangling B'rer Rabbit with a tar-baby, the practice of forcing the user to remain at a Web site on the Internet. When you try to leave the site by closing the browser window or typing in a new Web site address, the foot-in-the-door technique automatically opens a new browser window with a new Web site address, or simply disallows your leaving the site for a new one. Some mousetraps eventually run out of steam and permit you to break out after showing you a long series of new browser windows, while other mousetraps will continue opening new browser windows until you recall you can usually escape by typing Control-Alt-Delete. These technological tar-babies are a favorite of porn sites.

Movieokie　　In recent years this has become a favored form of karaoke among the computer-addicted who are also film buffs. It consists of acting out movie scenes while the backdrop is a silent rendition of the original film.

MUF　　A Department of Energy acronym for materials unaccounted for—the materials being special nuclear materials such as uranium and plutonium enriched to make a bomb.

Multicultural guidelines　　Diane Ravitch's *The Language Police* reports that educational publishers are increasingly using their pages to pursue goals other than the central goals of reading fluently or teaching science or math, but now "all this takes a backseat to social and political concerns." Thus, leading educational publishers judge textbook submissions against detailed multicultural guidelines, since "advocates of social change have set their sites on controlling reality by changing the way in which it is presented in textbooks."

Multiculturalism　　The celebration and respect for the pluralism of the diverse peoples, communities, ethnic and religious heritages, costumes, languages, folkways and mores of the many different immigrant and native groups in the country. The countervailing view debunks this notion, seeing multiculturalism as a denial of the need for rapid assimilation by newcomers gaining fluency in the English language and being mixed in the melting pot to accept the values, ideas and assumptions of those who have shaped American society and to which they have been drawn.

Mutual assured destruction   The consequence of this terrifying eventuality in a nuclear war has been frightening enough to prospective belligerents to stave off such a cataclysm for more than half a century.

My fellow Americans   Obligatory opening salvo in political addresses, followed by a stream of pious utterances and banal sloganeering.

Nannygate   The term for that increasingly common practice of candidates for high profile government office suddenly removing their name from consideration due to revelations about domestic help and usually, non-payment of Social Security and Medicare taxes. Variations, however, include Department of Labor Secretary designee (under Bush II) Linda Chavez, who "housed" an illegal immigrant, Attorney General nominee (under Clinton) Zoë Baird who failed to pay Social Security taxes for an illegal immigrant, Kimba Wood, who withdrew her name for nomination as Attorney General (under Clinton) when it was found she employed an undocumented worker, and in 2004 (under Bush II) Bernard Kerik, who withdrew his name from consideration for the head of the Department of Homeland Security over questions about the immigration status of his housekeeper-nanny.

NASCAR Dad   The kind of blue collar white male from the South or Midwest, who drives a pickup with a gun rack on the back window, country and western music blaring on the radio. Seen as a prototype by many: disaffected with politics and politicians and ready to vote for any candidate who speaks to his needs. Some think the Reagan Democrats personified this class of voters. NASCAR, of course, is the acronym for the National Association of Stock Car Racing.

Nation building   Too often this is the process of forcefully installing a government in a developing country that will support to the death

US interests. The term is also used as an expletive by many government bureaucrats, politicians and talk-show hosts who disdain the concept of pouring hard-earned "murican" dollars into a foreign rathole of health, education and infrastructure needs. Rather, if funds are to be expended, build up their security cadre to make the country safe for outsourcing.

National intelligence estimate   Reports from the professional intelligence community used by the George W. Bush Administration to justify the invasion of Iraq in 2003. The focus of the phrase has shifted from intelligence to estimate, since the Administration's searchers found no weapons of mass destruction.

Natural flavor   What this means is artificial flavor. Naturally!

Natural order   First advanced by Adam Smith in *The Wealth of Nations,* this late 18th century philosophy supported a private enterprise world market system, and it still acts as a theoretical foundation for the economics faculty of the University of Chicago.

Natural rate of unemployment   Seen by contemporary thinkers as that level of joblessness consistent with keeping the level of inflation close to the zero point, but seldom endorsed as natural by the jobless.

National security strategy   The doctrine enunciated by President George W. Bush at West Point on June 1, 2002, that the US would be prepared to take unilaterally determined preemptive military action whenever it feels itself threatened anywhere in the world as the Administration "rid[s] the world of evil."

Naval advanced logistic support site   What the Navy used to call a supply depot.

Need   Stir the word want into today's crucible of advertising messages and out it comes, transmogrified *to need.*

Needs work   An expression often heard by amateur writers and students who submit a truly unreadable manuscript. Also a real estate term for a wretched hovel.

Negative economic growth   This sounds infinitely more appealing than recession.

Negative employment growth   Hardly likely to mollify the anxieties of those affected by the more realistic word "unemployment."

Negative employee retention   A kinder, gentler term for firing workers.

Negative patient care outcome   In spite of the best public relations efforts the hospital industry can muster, no one is at all likely to be comforted by this way of characterizing a death.

Negatively privileged   A way for sociologists to not say poor people.

Negotiable   Real estate term meaning the seller forced the agent to list a house at that ridiculous price, but rationality may prevail in the end.

Neocon   Neo conservatism (the political position of those called Neocon). The term was invented by Michael Harrington to characterize some Republicans and Democrats in the late 1960s and 1970s who were anti-Communist and pro-Western in their views. Later Neocons were thought to be staunchly against the government's regulation of business and in favor of welfare reform. Today this loosely defined group is strongly behind transformation of the world, based upon a strong moral conviction about the rightness of America in its battle against evil. Even though their historically liberal antecedents may have been supporters of the New Deal, current Neocons are typically defined as reactionary foreign policy hawks who are disposed to bring freedom and democracy to foreign nations even when it takes a preemptive military assault. The word is also the description for the influential and articulate advisers and officials in the Pentagon and the White House.

Neoconomy   A term coined by Harvard-educated economist and New York Times columnist Daniel Altman in his 2004 book, *Neoconomy, George Bush's Revolutionary Gamble with America's Future*. Altman suggests that the Bush II economic agenda is set on transforming the American economy—not counting the long-term impact of the biggest deficit in history—to change the way we finance our government. Increased savings would usher in this golden age of neoconomy. With those tax cuts, we are expected to put those funds into investments such as stocks and bonds and mutual funds. Those savings are supposed to rev up our economic engine. Never mind that the competition for what's left in our wallet would have an average of four hours a day of TV broadcasts suggesting terrific things we need to buy rather than save the money, that we would have no social safety net and the poor and the rich would live in two separate and unequal cocoons. There is also an assumption by neoconimists that investments would flow into American corporations, but it is just as likely the funds will rush to better deals abroad and that rising government deficits will pluck any excess bucks from your wallet as the dollar's value shrinks. There could also be some hard feelings by the working stiffs who are paying the bills for the fire department, military, medical research and education when they find out that their rich neighbors across the tracks are paying no income tax at all, since they are living off tax-free investments.

Neo-creo   Relying on the intellect and science instead of the bible as a source, individuals of this persuasion, termed neo-creationism or the intelligent design movement, hold to the conviction that human life is far too complex to have resulted simply through the process of evolution.

Networking   Among the more pervasive and sympathetic meanings of this word, now in widespread use, is the reference to Internet-based relationships which share information thorough a kind of human brokerage to aid your search for Mr. or Ms. Right. Another use of the term applies to the activity of maintaining or expanding personal social connections and ties among friends and business associates as well as other forms of human interactions and interdependencies.

Never needs ironing   New wrinkle-free fabrics proclaiming this feature often announce, in the small print, that this feature applies only if you follow a specific laundering regimen. Other clothes with this feature are particularly appealing to those who would not iron their clothes in any event, or glance at the mirror without their glasses.

New age   The way to describe the broad trends which define alternative approaches to traditional cultural norms. The movement is particularly involved with spiritual exploration and holistic medicine, providing iconoclastic views of philosophy, religion, science, music and life styles. New age religious convictions are a mix of spiritual beliefs which often combine Christian faith with ideas drawn from other cultures such as reincarnation, rebirth, and sometimes belief in the magical, mystical and other-worldly phenomena.

New economy   From the mid 1990s to the end of the decade, the US economy bloomed, fertilized by the Internet and new information technology. That heady growth, with stock values doubling, resembled the hothouse economy of the post-WW II period. The growth spurt lasted until the millennium, when what was heralded as the beginning of a new era—"the new economy"—began to wilt, and is now characterized as no more than a garden-variety anomaly, a frenetic hyperactive period that has occurred from time to time, almanacs tell us, for more than 200 years.

New federalism   A governmental form of hot-potato in which programs and their benefits are precipitously tossed to state and local governments by the Feds. When state and local governments suddenly acquire the responsibility for administering the programs and paying out benefits, Congress overlooked one key element, passing on to the state and local governments the funds needed to pay for them. The Bush II Administration has made massive reductions in financial support for those delegated programs, leaving state and local governments staring incredulously into their empty coffers.

New world order   In a long forgotten phrase, Bush I proclaimed that the Gulf War has been fought on behalf of "a new world order," a phrase first used by Woodrow Wilson to define his proposed peace settlement after the First World War. In a way, a new world order did come into existence when Bush II's Iraq War divided the world into a handful of countries that supported his preemptive strike, and the vast majority of the nations of the world, that did not.

Next Gens   Some call this segment of the American people, made up of those born between 1982 and 2002, Millenniums. With their number at 81 million, they form the greatest population group since the Baby Boomers, estimated at 87 million.

Nicotine nazis   A term manufactured by pro-smoking spin-doctors to indicate those "anti-tobacco operatives," who enforce regulations combating the spread of lung cancer and heart disease.

Nicotini   With indoor smoking banished so widely across the land, this cocktail that contains the key element of the addictive weed is now served in some bars to placate the longings of the tobacco-deprived.

NIMBY   Acronym for Not In My Back Yard, a battle cry in neighborhoods fighting any manner of plans to change the character of their area, be it by polluting industries, the construction of a firehouse, hospital or prison, halfway house, mall or high rise apartments.

No brainer   A term suggesting the solution is not going to tax your IQ, or that there is an obvious, simple solution.

No child left behind   The slogan used to characterize the provision embodied in the No Child Left Behind Act (drawn from the Children's Defense Fund's mission statement) and promoted by the George W. Bush Administration to ensure meaningful school choice by providing access to information based upon standardized testing, which would allow parents to compare programs and hold schools accountable for results. Under the act's provisions children are expected to be tested annually from third through eighth grade in math and reading. Students in schools that fail to measure up will have the ability to choose other schools in the same district. Obstacles to actually helping students receive a better education through this program are, first, there must indeed be a school in the district that is performing up to par to which a student could transfer, and second, there is a multi-million dollar shortfall in federal funding to actually support this legislation. The Bush II guidelines for the 2006 budget, for example, include a $1.7 billion cut for education. Head Start faces a cut of $100 million in the same budget proposal.

No problem   Today's stylized response to a request in a restaurant or at a service counter. In more gracious times, the response was "of course" or "I'd be delighted." No problem is a way of raising the status of the responder from servant, paid to take care of your needs, to a functionary who evaluates your request and after careful consideration, foresees no immediate obstacle in actually consenting to it.

NOAEL *see* **LOAEL**

Non-believer   A host of textbook publishers have banned *heathen* as ethnocentric, asking their writers to replace it with this term.

Non-multicolor capability   A rather roundabout way of describing a black and white television screen.

Non-performing credits   If at the annual stockholder's meeting of, say, a bank, you hear their treasurer mentioning this term, just jot down that they lost money in bad loans and debts. A variant of the term is non-performing assets. The treasurer dismisses these losses as "rolling over or rescheduling" and dang it but that has contributed to a "negative contribution to profits." If the treasurer is white haired and particularly distinguished in appearance, he may get away with the term "net profit revenue deficiency" with a straight face.

Nonmarital birth   An out-of-wedlock birth.

Not for attribution   A masking term for not disclosing the name of the individual who provided the information used in the media accounts of the story. While the purpose of such a process is to provide reliable background information on an issue, it can also be used to whisper disclosures though a knothole in the government's bureaucratic wall.

Not quite ready for prime time   A less than professional production.

Not really   How youth express a negative evaluation.

Nuclear accident   A more straightforward, albeit understated term for technological failure, often coupled with human error, that threatens public health and the environment. Such problems occur on a routine basis, be they melting fuel elements, coolant leaks, radiation leakage, radioactive contamination of workers or aircraft or submarine accidents.

Nuclear event   An atomic explosion or leak of radioactivity, using language to make it sound like a celebration.

Nuclear option   Republicans have been threatening a procedural maneuver known in Washington parlance as the nuclear option. This requires a change in the rules of the Senate, advanced by the Senate Majority Leader Dr. William Frist, which would effectively bar Democrats from unlimited debate—filibustering—any appointments, particularly judicial nominations. The convoluted path to the present problem can be traced back to President Lyndon Johnson's nominating Justice Abe Fortas to succeed Chief Justice Warren. Republicans joined Southern Democrats in using the Senate's tradition of unlimited debate to prevent a floor vote and with two-thirds majority needed to stop a filibuster, the proposed nomination died a quiet death. This filibuster technique allowed the Senate to block two Nixon nominations as well as Reagan's nomination of Robert Bork. Blocking candidates in this fashion worked so well that the process was used to block lower court nominees as well. Thus, when Republicans gained control of the Senate under Clinton, they shot down many of his federal court nominations, followed by Democrats blocking votes on 10 of Bush II's nominees to federal appeals courts. Thus the filibustering and the proposed "nuclear option" of having Vice President Cheney, in his capacity as the Senate's presiding officer, make a judgment, flying in the face of Senate tradition, that it will take but a simple majority of voting senators to close debate and thus stop a filibuster on a judicial nomination. Critics point out that if the filibuster disappears, there would be no check on the President's ability to put anyone on the courts. Even some Republican senators do not support this change on the practical grounds that what goes around comes around; the next time the Republicans are the minority party in the Senate, there would be no check on Democratic nominations. Further, as Republican Senator John McCain has observed, the Framers of the Constitution meant the minority in the Senate to have influence in the proceedings. Robert Byrd, former Democratic majority leader observed in March 2005, "If senators are denied their right of free speech on judicial nominations, an attack on extended debate on all other matters cannot be far behind. This would mean no leverage for the minority to effect compromise, and no bargaining power for individual senators as they strive to represent the people of their states."

Nukespeak Jargon used to hide the devastating destructive force of nuclear weapons by employing everyday language and bureaucratic evasion in a non-threatening manner in public discourse, as evidenced by the term "Peacekeeper" used in the Reagan Administration when speaking of a class of deadly missiles.

Nutraceuticals The word to describe all the things other than regular food that people consume in the pursuit of good health. They can be in foods which contain "added" vitamins, sports drinks, water, and even in some candy. They also include multivitamins, weight loss cures and herbal preparations. It is estimated that six-in-ten American adults consume one or more such supplements daily.

OBE An acronym meaning (1) an out-of-body-experience to Tibetan scholars, (2) outcome-based-education to the National Education Association, (3) the Order of the British Empire—used to celebrate outstanding achievements—to General George Patton, Steven Spielberg, and Pelé, all recipients, or (4) overcome by events by State Department bureaucrats.

Occupational stereotyping A major school text publisher's guidelines warn against "showing people in roles that are commonly experienced in reality." Thus, remember, it is stereotyping to show Asian Americans working in a laundry, men appearing as plumbers or women portrayed as nurses and receptionists.

Off the record The comments by politicians and government officials to journalists, with the proviso that their words may not be used. Breach of this trust by journalists is viewed as a cardinal sin.

OGA An acronym for "other government agency" used in the military to refer to the Central Intelligence Agency. While the Bush II Administration insisted that all prisoners captured in Iraq were covered by the Geneva Conventions, dozens of "OGA" prisoners were kept off the prisoner rosters and transferred to Guantanamo and other interrogation sites to hide them from Red Cross inspectors, according to two US Army generals, testifying before a Congressional committee in September 2004.

WEASEL WORDS O

Old Europe   A term of derision coined by Bush II's Secretary of Defense, Donald Rumsfeld, to describe America's erstwhile allies, the nations of Western Europe, for refusing to support militarily the US crusade against Iraq.

Older persons   This is acceptable in American educational textbooks, but they warn against using *aged*. It is unlikely an educational publisher, however, would accept the descriptive phrase, "a person older than God."

On hold   What happens when you finally reach an operator in a company that proclaims "your call is important to us" (see entry) or under-funded government agencies that offer a phone-in service and proclaim, "we're there for you," with their token phone-answering specialist. The term is also used in government circles to mean that for political or financial reasons or both, they have no intention of pursuing the project, enforcing the regulation, or considering the option.

On sale   The most ubiquitous and meaningless expression in retailing. Such a claim in an ad, store window or attached to an item is viewed with skepticism by any but the most innocent shopper since it seems everything is always on sale. The word goes hand in glove with the hollow exclamation, Save!

On task   A person or group focused on productive, agreed-upon goals.

One hundred and ten percent   A term often heard tripping from the lips of sports newscasters meaning a highly motivated effort that causes listening math teachers to involuntarily grind their teeth.

One nation, under God   Ceremonial deism which has found its way into the lines of the Pledge of Allegiance. The constitutionality of the words "under God" was litigated all the way to the US Supreme Court, where it was sanctified in 2004.

One per customer   Either rationing at near cost of a newly introduced product, or still another Madison Avenue ploy to create a sense of scarcity for a product they want to unload.

One size fits all   Either there is an elastic quality in the product, or the product, such as an apron, is simply longer and shorter on the wearer, or the company has, with a transmogrification device, over-come the demographic bell-shaped curve of sizes.

Operation Desert Storm   The first Bush Presidency's designation for the 1991 war with Iraq.

Optimist   The American Institutes for Research want you to use this term rather than Pollyanna, which they suggest is sexist.

Organization chart   A diagram that represents the parts of a com-pany or government agency, as well as personnel titles and reporting relationships. These charts display a view of reality akin to the last line of *The Sun Also Rises:* "Isn't it pretty to think so?"

Organoleptic analysis   The term is used in evaluating everything from frozen fish to wine. If you sniff fish and it smells to high heaven, then the fish has failed its organoleptic analysis. If you send off a wine to be evaluated by a specialist, you certainly would not want to spend all that money for a wine sniffer, would you?

Outplacement consultant   No longer drawing a paycheck due to the "rightsizing" of your former company? You might want to check in with this person, who in olden times was called an unemployment counselor.

Outside the box   Thinking up unconventional and original strate-gies when an individual or organization is faced with a problem or a challenge.

Outsourcing   The practice of companies moving their production abroad to use low-cost foreign workers rather than keeping their operation here and paying US wages. The practice started by replac-ing foreign workers for Americans to assemble US made products, moved on to those workers producing the goods, and now includes distance neutral products such as customer-service reps and com-puter programmers. *See also Insourcing.*

Overmature trees   A fox-eyeing-henhouse-chickens term used by lumber companies and members of the US Forest Service for long-standing, healthy trees they view as ready to be cut down.

Overconnectedness   The passion among those in society who can-not bear to cut the cord of their ever-increasing ties via cell phones and portable electronic instruments.

Ownership society Like many politically charged terms, it depends if you are looking at the bulges in our balloon of taxes or the hand squeezing it. Bush II's use of this phrase means the reduction or elimination of taxes on savings and investments, including capital gains, on stocks, bonds and real estate. The owners of these investments would be untaxed on their resources. A nifty idea, right, to support home ownership and tax-sheltered savings? Not quite. If you choke off that revenue source, our national tax burden has to be carried by wages and salaries—a wage tax. That means your weekly pay packet, after you pay for the entire operation of the government, would not really leave much for food and stuff like that, what with ever-increasing health costs and pension payments. Many of the wealthy could live tax free off their investments, allowing working stiffs to keep the government operating.

P

PACs   The French version of a man and a woman living with each other short of matrimony. The *pacte civile de solidarité* provides an alternative to the marital state. This "conventional marriage light" involves a legal process providing the couple many of the rights of married people without committing them to remain together. While the George W. Bush Administration proposed the US government fund methods to encourage marriage, European countries are finding pragmatic ways to grant legal status to couples unwilling to go as far as wedlock.

Painting a house   The colorful language of the Mafia for murdering someone, based upon the graphic scene of blood spattering all over the walls as a result.

Paper or plastic?   A term of greeting at check-out counters, referencing your preference in grocery bags. Historians claim that in ancient times, when you approached a counter, a civil greeting was provided, often including a query about your health or your family.

Parade of horribles   A phrase meaning a series of unhappy events in dust-jacket talk, as well as a term used to describe a listing of anticipated negative results, as identified by a pessimist or possibly a realist.

Partial birth abortion   Coined by the pro-life movement for a procedure for abortions done in the third trimester of pregnancy, what the American College of Obstetrics and Gynecology defines as intact dilation and extraction, where the fetus has grown too large to fit easily through the woman's higher cervix. A bill, passed by Congress and signed into law by George W. Bush in October 2003, outlaws this practice, but the legality of the measure is being challenged by opponents who view it as a part of the movement to restrict abortion step by step in a battle to sway public opinion against the 1973 *Roe v. Wade* court decision that recognized the legal right to abort.

Passenger facility charge A new way to describe a tax imposed upon airline passengers.

Patriot Act The measure passed in October 2001, "uniting and strengthening America by providing appropriate tools required to intercept and obstruct terrorism," or the US Patriot Act. Critical reaction to this law has grown as the media report the denial of civil liberties guaranteed under the Bill of Rights, and instances of what are viewed to be unbridled and contemptuous assaults on individual rights related to the detention of thousands of people by the Attorney General without charging them with any crime, and the closing of immigration hearings that were formerly public. Of late, Congressional modifications have shown some sensitivity to civil liberties issues, zapping a plan that would have allowed the general public to fink on their neighbor's suspicious activities, a national identification card and a plan for big brother to scan computer databases to spot suspected terrorists. With Attorney General John Ashcroft departed, however, there has been no change. The Department of Justice is using these new powers in ordinary criminal cases. Even the inspector general for the department, joining a host of others, found serious flaws in the treatment of detainees.

Paula Principle *see* **Peter Principle**

Pay-per-click *see* **Click-through**

Peace dividend The benefits that had been expected to accrue to American citizens through the reduction in military expenditures, which would reduce taxes and permit increased expenditures on social programs once the Cold War ended. The phrase was coined by Columbia University professor Seymour Melman. The expectations proved short-lived. Post-1989 events in the Balkans and elsewhere drew US military responses, and once again, the taxpayer was stuck with these new expenditures, costs that matched or were higher than the Cold War era.

Peace process The actions that the government undertakes in any area of the world where American involvement is characterized as working toward reducing conflict or furthering peace, even when our participation fails to either end hostilities or restore stability to the region.

Peaceful coexistence The notion that governments that hold convictions which are conflicting can manage to survive tranquilly with each other by accepting or ignoring their differences in the interest of stability.

Peacekeepers Soldiers who serve as an occupying force in a foreign country. Also a weapon of mass destruction developed for the United States, and the plural of the Pentagon's Peacekeeper, a four-stage intercontinental ballistic missile capable of spreading atomic devastation to 10 separate cities. Starting in 1948, the US built over 300 B-36s for nuclear delivery, a six-engine jet designated the Peacemaker.

Pearl tea A refreshing cold shake served in Asian snack shops. The drink contains tea, ice, and milk which you drink from wide straws since, as you will immediately discover, the other ingredient is tapioca "pearls" the size and texture of frog's eyeballs, which you suck upwards from the depths of the drink.

People of the United States Several educational publishers' writer's guidelines suggest its writers employ this term, rather than 'Americans', which suggests 'geographical chauvinism.' It is our guess that such writers do not hang out in VFW bars.

People's democracy Or People's Republic or People's Democratic Republic as they are sometimes called, implies that sovereignty flows from the people to the government. It turns out, sadly, that virtually all such governments are led by a supreme head of state or oligarchy with all the characteristics of a communist or socialist state.

People who are blind The term *the blind* is banned as offensive by a host of educational publishers; you are asked to replace it with this phrase instead.

Perfectly clear *see* **Making things perfectly clear**

Permanent global summer season The abundant availability of fresh fruits and vegetables for sale in retail stores year round, as a result of the way in which the food industry buys and distributes produce from all over the world.

Permission marketing Or 'opt-in email', a term referencing those companies you welcome—or at least grudgingly accept—information from, such as an Internet security company, a newspaper whose daily Internet updates you scan, or those utilities you sent in a warranty for. A pleasanter example would be a neighborhood bookstore that lets you know when they have a book they think you will be interested in reading, or on a grander scale, Amazon's profiling of your interests based on past purchases.

Perp-walk An abridgement of perpetrator's walk. With hands and feet shackled, that ubiquitous shot of someone charged with a criminal offense, escorted by deputies positioned to provide TV news a clear shot, as the accused and his escorts make their way to a courtroom to face charges.

Persistency specialist Late in paying your credit card bill? You might be hearing from someone with this title, rather than that much blunter term, bill collector.

Person who can't hear or speak A host of educational publishers ask its writers to use this term rather than deaf-mute.

Person who is non-disabled A major educational publisher suggests using this phrase rather than *able-bodied*, and to never use the term *abnormal* as it is demeaning to persons with disabilities.

Person who is mobility impaired This is how at least two educational publishers want their writers to refer to people who use a wheelchair.

Person who has arthritis Somehow this sounds better than "arthritic patient" to at least one educational textbook publisher.

Personal preservation flotation device What you had better cling to in order to save yourself from drowning. If in a hurry just grab a life preserver.

Pessimist The American Institutes for Research, a non-profit organization of applied research, wants us to use this term as a politically correct substitute for Cassandra, the daughter of King Priam of Troy, whose ability to see into the future of her dad's kingdom kept her from being overly optimistic.

Pessimists and naysayers   A term used by White House Press Secretary Scott McClellan, in September 2004, to characterize the increasing number of CIA and other intelligence specialists who believe the Bush II Iraq policy was digging itself ever deeper into a sandy quagmire.

Pest control technician   An exterminator, in the 19th century, known as a rat catcher.

Peter principle   The notion that every person in an organization, whether business or government, rises to his or her level of incompetence and remains entrenched there forever more. The concept was an observation of Laurence Peters, a Canadian educator in the 1960s, but the idea strikes a chord with anyone who toils in a bureaucracy. The inverse is the Paula Principle, which holds that women in organizations are mired below their level of competence—perhaps as a consequence of being seen as threatening to their less competent male peers.

Phishing   A scam, also known as brand spoofing, because the perpetrators disguise themselves as being a well known business, such as a bank or a credit card company, and approach prospective victims through unsolicited emails seeking to entice them into revealing personal financial information. These details then make it possible to steal identities and run up credit card charges or order new credit cards. It is very difficult for consumers to deal with such a dodge because it's virtually impossible to know by looking at the message whether it is genuine or not.

Phone ladies   The women in rural towns in India and Bangladesh who set themselves up in a small business by buying an inexpensive cell phone and renting it to their phoneless neighbors.

Phood   In light of stagnant or declining sales, companies in the food industry are turning to the manufacture of "phoods:" nutritionally enhanced products intersecting food and pharmaceutical content. The plan is to appeal to the ever-growing number of health-conscious consumers, particularly since they will pay more for dietary fare which provides health benefits such as lowering cholesterol or improving digestion. *See also Neutraceuticals*

Photo op   An abridgment of photo opportunity, this is arranged for the press and media by staff assistants to political figures or celebrities in order to set up a scene designed to appear natural during which the subject is seen doing or saying something ostensibly newsworthy.

Physical attribute of abilities stereotyping   An educational test publisher's guidelines warn about references to group stereotypes. They must make certain that there are no references to African Americans being good at sports, or that men are strong, that women are overly concerned about their appearance or that older people are ever feeble.

Physical pressure   Police or military torture of prisoners.

Physically challenged   A proper rendition for characterizing individuals who are in some way handicapped or limited in their mobility. The term handicapped evolved from the 18th century term "hand in cap," referring to a game of chance whereby one challenged another for some article to exchange. It evolved into a racing term, in which the horse judged superior was given added weight to allow the lesser competitor a sporting chance. Thus, by definition, a handicapped person was presumed superior and needing some sort of alteration to level the playing field for the competition.

Pioneer   This is the politically correct term to use in educational textbooks, not *backwoodsman*.

Plain paper wrapper   The preferred term of concealment for the mailing of "sensual products" to your residence.

Plan B   The name given to the use of the morning-after pill, taken by women to avoid conception.

Plant superintendent   In other days known simply as a janitor.

Platform plank   Righteous bromides impossible to contradict, intended to support the electability of the person professing those views.

Plausible denial   Official government lies that result when incomplete statements are made, false documents are substituted for genuine ones or true documents are simply destroyed so that evidence is made to vanish—all in order to mislead those seeking the truth.

Pocket call   What happens when a person's cell phone bumps into something and hits the buttons to accidentally ring a number.

Podcast   A recording that is uploaded onto a Web site and then downloaded on an iPod or any MP3 player. The term combines iPod and broadcasting. This process, started in 2004, differs from broadcasting in that the recording—which often is produced daily—can be automatically sent to the listener's computer or iPod and played at the convenience of the listener, who is not constrained by broadcast schedules. Bloggers discovered that this allows them to produce and distribute audio files via their Web sites, hence their increasing popularity.

PODS   In the past the term has meant Proof of Delivery Systems, Principles of Database Systems, or a social group of whales, but recently, thanks to our consumer culture, when your house can't hold all the stuff you bought—or because of a renovation project—we have the newest use of the term: trailer-size plywood containers, sheeted with aluminum. These storage bins, their name an acronym for Portable On Demand Storage, are sprouting up across America. Companies drop them off on driveways and lawns, while scowling neighbors mutter about eyesores and the need for regulations on how long they can stay at a residential property.

Poison pill   The deliberate strategy used by a company under siege by prospective take-over firms to make it less of an appealing acquisition target for the unwanted predator by taking on liabilities or establishing other roadblocks, which would sharply deter such suitors.

Police action   Description applied by a government which, without formal declaration of war, carries out military assaults by their regular armed forces against those whom they or a country they support, or defends against guerrillas, terrorists or insurrection fighters in a foreign country or region because they view such combatants to be in violation of national or international peace and order. The term was first used by the US during the Truman presidency to characterize the Korean War.

Policy wonk   The word *wonk* has its origin as a disparaging way to define a studious or zealously hardworking person, a sort of first cousin to the term egghead. The combination of policy with wonk, according to some, was brought to Washington by Harvard alumni who put the two words together to mean someone with an obsessive preoccupation with every last detail of public policy issues. The dilemma for policy wonks running for office is to conceal their depth of knowledge on an issue since discussing a topic with all its ramifications causes confusion to audiences and frustrates our sound-bite-driven media.

Pollution rights   Proprietary rights of companies with unused allowances to pollute the environment to sell those rights to other companies who can then blithely emit their own legally purchased ration of toxins. The Bush II White House continued to enlarge such rights in this pay-to-sin program invented way back in the Reagan years.

Poor   Those the far right dismisses as the under-motivated and welfare-greedy portion of society.

Poorly buffered precipitation   If acid rain sounds too appalling perhaps this phrase can do the job of explaining it.

Pop   Hip hop for shooting at someone.

Pop-up ad   Advertisements that jump on your computer screen like a jack-in-the-box from hell. These uninvited interventions into your Web-browsing have spawned a number of "pop-up killer software" programs to counter them.

Porno-chic   Today's outpouring of sexually explicit lingerie available in many mainstream stores featuring thongs, brassieres, panties and garter belts that are marketed to the fashion conscious in suggestive advertising and would-you-believe-it displays.

Pornosophy   The term characterizing the remarkable act of sexual coupling while simultaneously reflecting upon scientific or philosophical questions.

Portal shields   Military terminology for biological detection systems that operate at installations in the Persian Gulf region.

Portfolio administrator   The language of our time for bill collectors.

Positive discrimination   "L'affirmative action" in America connotes to many in France an ill-conceived contrivance that they believe deepens societal divisions. Such programs are impossible in France since their census tables do not collect data on race, ethnicity or religion. Therefore the French translate the concept to mean positive discrimination.

Possibly When CIA analysts use this term, it indicates they believe there is less than a 50 percent chance the hypothesis is valid.

Post-bubble anxiety disorder This is how the severe money concerns resulting from the market tailspin at the end of the 1990s have been characterized.

Post-crash realism The far more balanced perspective that has replaced the ubiquitous earlier euphoria, which held the computer industry in its thrall in the months before the stock market nosedive.

Post-modern churches Several hundred small evangelical congregations have been forming in recent years to express an alternative form of worship. Diverse in their theology, they meet in nontraditional settings, their congregants often loosely linked through Internet sites, Web logs and conferences. They are also known as emerging churches.

Postmortem divorce The characterization for the way an unhappily married Japanese woman uses clandestine means to arrange for her burial elsewhere than at her husband's side.

Post-trauma job changer Those who elect to switch to a more socially valued or rewarding career choice after they have been psychologically influenced by a personal event in their lives, or some phenomenon like 9/11, which fundamentally revises their personal outlook.

Potentially disruptive re-entry system Department of Defense talk for the Titan II nuclear-armed intercontinental ballistic missile.

Potomac fever An infectious disease that affects aspirants to federal offices, particularly Presidential hopefuls. It is believed the illness is transmitted by inhaling the beguiling vapors of the river flowing through Washington, DC.

Pouch Or diplomatic pouch. A State Department term for heavy canvas or plastic bags containing mail, equipment or supplies sent to overseas posts. Classified pouches contain official communications and travel under the watchful control of a diplomatic courier, who keeps an eye on the bags from start to finish, including last-on, first-off international flights. Pouches enjoy diplomatic protection and thus are exempt from foreign customs searches. Diplomats often use the term as a verb, "to pouch this back to Washington," for example. The bags are large enough to have been used as an informal method of egress from a country.

Poverty of values   A term then-Vice President Dan Quayle employed in his righteous finger-pointing at sitcom Murphy Brown's being an unwed mother.

Power alley   The expression for the aisle leading in from the entrance in a discount store or supermarket.

Power lunch   The term for political operatives, and to a lesser degree, industry biggies, who meet over lunch at a trendy watering hole, particularly an establishment hangout within hopping distance to the Capitol.

Power walking   A form of exercise practiced by people who look best not dressed in form-fitting clothes, which involves rigorous arm waving and marching associated with that final shot in grainy films showing the Royal Fusiliers quick-stepping into Lhasa.

Power partners *see* **Climate leaders**

Power rudeness   Inconsiderate personal behavior by those who receive cell phone calls and use their beepers in public places, like restaurants and movies, to the consternation of those around them.

PPC *see* **Click-through**

Preassembled furniture   These are benches, bookcases and similar items that come in a cardboard box with a picture of the item in its final assembled glory. Included is a simple diagram for construction showing, after repeated study of the simple diagram, that you placed part c in a part d site, requiring a rebuilding of the item one more time. The genius of industrial design is once again proven to be not the finished product, but the skill with which all the components can be stuffed into one compact box.

Pre-dawn vertical insertion   The picturesque military term for the American armed parachute invasion of Grenada.

WEASEL WORDS

Preemptive counterattack A Department of Defense term for the process of the United States attacking a state to counter what could be an attack on the United States. Of course, after the attack on the other state, it is useful in a democracy to find some sort of valid supporting evidence, something the Bush II Administration is learning.

Pre-existing condition Not a term used to explain predestination, but rather found on any medical insurance application. It means a medical condition for which you have received treatment or should receive treatment, which in turn raises your premiums even higher, or in some cases, is exempted from coverage.

Pre-feminist The era predating the modern feminist cultural movement, when women were ostensibly content with the role of wife, mother and homemaker as their paramount societal contribution.

Pre-owned Second hand, or perhaps fourth hand, but distinctly not new. Still, if you are buying a Mercedes, it somehow sounds better.

Prekindergarten What used to be called a nursery school has evolved into a prep school for kindergarten, enrolling children under age 5.

Premature antifascist Label applied to American and British volunteers who, in the 1930s, fought against General Franco's forces during the Spanish Civil War.

Premium practice Patients who pay a doctor a substantial annual membership fee are entitled to special preferential treatment under the terms of this questionable system—also known as "boutique health care."

Premiums A mandatory payment proposed by then President Clinton to pay for a proposed health plan, otherwise known as a tax.

Prenup In a time when fully 50 percent of all marriages end in divorce, it is little wonder that the pre-nuptial legal document, which spells out the practical details of the description of the partners' property, has become much more commonplace. And while there's nothing romantic about the prenup, legal conflicts during a divorce proceeding aren't very romantic either.

Preschool In olden days, when parents wore hats and school desks had inkwells, the term meant that your kids were too young to go to school. No more. It has evolved into the starting blocks of readiness training in your child's competitive race to post-doctoral training at Harvard Medical School. Long gone is the idea of nursery school, which connotes wasteful hours at play, not ticking off key "learning outcomes" for young Tyler's competitive advancement.

Presenteeism   A term for those fellow workers who show up for work while sick either because they lose income if they stay home or for less understandable reasons. Of course, coming to work sick jeopardizes the health of others, and recent studies suggest this is causing an estimated annual $150 billion loss in productivity in the United States.

Preventive detention   This was a well-known practice of Nazi Germany, pre-Mandela South Africa, and in other totalitarian regimes, whereby people are locked up due to suspected political association, or racial, religious or ethnic identity. Bush II's former Attorney General, John Ashcroft, initiated America's third such activity of preventive detention after the terrorist attacks of September 11, 2001. By January 2004, over 5,000 foreign nationals, "suspected terrorists," were placed behind bars. Prior mass detentions have proven as unsuccessful as Ashcroft's: none of his detainees have been found to have contributed to the al Qaeda September 11 attacks, only three have been charged with terrorist crimes, and two of those three were acquitted, leaving one lone conviction tainted with charges the principal prosecution witness lied on the stand. Thus the batting average of zero for three in American detention campaigns. Following the 1919 terrorist bombings in eight US cities, several thousand foreign nationals were rounded up by the Justice Department. Hundreds were deported. No links to the bombings were found. During World War II, 110,000 persons, both US citizens and foreign nationals, were interned in camps because of their Japanese ancestry. No links were found to espionage or sabotage, the reason given for their incarceration.

Preventive sanctions   Legal punitive actions designed to dissuade an individual or organization from a specific course of action, or to prevent other parties from pursuing the same course of action. This type of measure is applied in corporate, governmental and political contexts.

Price enhancement   A stealth term for an increase in how much it costs to buy something.

Price points   What a customer is going to be charged for an item, given the tug of war between profit and what the merchant believes the patron is willing to fork out.

Price supports   Government subsidies provided to maintain the prices of farm products at a certain prescribed level. If the market price falls below this level for particular crops or dairy products farmers receive "deficiency payments" to make up the difference. A more subtle type of support takes the form of tariffs on particular farm products to contain the flow of cheaper–priced foreign imports. Consumer and free trade advocates decry both tactics as causing American consumers to pay higher prices for food products than would be the case if true market competition rather than price supports or import tariffs were in effect.

Prioritize   A modern term for the process of rank ordering by importance. In political jargon it means to dismiss or ignore items low down on the totem pole and possibly to address some of the top-ranked items.

Pro-choice   The term for the belief in legalized abortion.

Pro-flag, -children, -environment   Republican Minority Whip, Newt Gingrich, included this term in his booklet, "Language, a Key Mechanism of Control," which he mailed in 1990 to Republican leaders across America. The booklet contained a list of "vivid, brilliant" positive words he suggested they use to characterize Republicans and negative words to describe their Democrat opponents. The positive list included this term.

Pro-life   The rallying cry of anti-abortionists in support of the fetus, with distinctly less passion in evidence for the quality of life once the child is among the living.

Product placement   The tactic of ensuring that a particular branded product is inserted, or advertisers would prefer to say, integrated, into a film or television production, in a strategic place where it is certain to be noticed by the viewers.

Progressive taxes   The idea that the federal tax requirements should obligate the rich to pay a higher proportionate rate than the less affluent. But the tax on income during the Bush II Administration has become distinctly unprogressive with the wealthiest taxpayers enjoying the lion's share of the reductions in the proportion of their income paid in taxes.

Protest zones In order to recognize the rights of protesters, prescribed areas are established by the police in order that those exercising their right of free speech can be controlled in a roped-off zone. Typically the protesters are placed far enough away from the event so that their voices do not drown out the speaker's voice or otherwise interfere with the proceedings.

Public broadcasting Modestly funded national radio and television networks with local affiliates scattered throughout the country that are dependent in large measure upon contributions from subscribers, foundations, corporate sponsors and paid advertising. Founded to provide access to public service programming less likely to attract commercial sponsorship, financial considerations, competitive zeal and narrow audience appeal is propelling public broadcasters, more and more, toward many of the characteristics of the commercial marketplace.

Public diplomacy This differs from the traditional forms of diplomacy conducted by US officials in that it refers to government-supported cultural, educational and media efforts to explain to the rest of the world what American policies, practices and culture are all about. It takes innumerable forms including educational, literary and artistic exchange activities, television and radio broadcasts and journalistic and public affairs programs. Its strength resides in the way it presents many different views because it reaches out to foreign audiences with a pluralistic message from American publishing, academia and the arts, not simply echoing official US government positions.

Public interest The idea that there are some types of measures that benefit the community as a whole and that may be affected by government or private actions. These are matters that bear upon the general public's concerns, or the condition of the natural world and the environment, rather than the interests of any individual or small number of people or special groups at the expense of the many. Put another way, this term describes efforts deemed to support public or civic causes in opposition to corporate or private advantages. The debate inevitably devolves into a catfight from various factions as to what is in the public interest.

Public waste reception area The odor and sight of the garbage dump are scarcely ameliorated by the terminology.

Pulse An inside-the-beltway term for pestering, as in "why don't you pulse the Department of Justice about that?"

Pundit Someone who is viewed by the media, and thus it follows by the public, as having great insight, expertise and/or special experience, which qualifies that person to render authoritative opinions and judgments about political matters and public events. The process of punditry, of expressing such views as a columnist or commentator, derives from the Hindi word pandit. Pundits, alas, are often decidedly wrong in their pronouncements, to the delight of innumerable skeptics.

Punitive sanctions Penalties imposed by a government upon nations with whom the Administration is in open disagreement over such issues as military differences, suspected acts of terrorism or the harboring of terrorists. They take the form of imposing export and import trade embargoes on companies and individuals who might do business with such nations and by making travel to and from such countries unlawful. The US has targeted in this way such countries as Cuba, Syria, North Korea, Burma and Libya. Critics reason that while multilateral sanctions may have an impact, unilateral sanctions hurt only the poor of the targeted nations and often strengthen the power of despots.

Purple state *see* **Red state**

Quaint   A real estate term meaning small, old, and eccentric in structure or setting.

Quality time   Given the economic realities of wage-earning in America, there is little time for enjoying your immediate family or significant others. Thus, this term has come to mean the cherished moments when you actually spend time with those you love, and those you have a sense of obligation to spend non-work related time with, other than while car-pooling or over a hastily consumed meal.

Quick and dirty   An inelegant, often temporary, solution to a problem.

R

Racial privacy   A 2003 California constitutional ballot initiative that lost. It would have required that "the state shall not classify any individual by race, ethnicity, color or national origin in the operation of public education, public contracting or public employment." If it had won, according to opponents of the initiative, it would have erased information needed to assess discrimination, health issues, hate crimes and sectors of student populations. Proponents suggested it would lessen the racial balkanization of America and lead to healthy "color-blindness."

Racist   A term used for those charged with demeaning or discriminating against members of racial groups by their utterances, through political tactics, by unfair treatment in the workplace and educational institutions and through symbolic use of racial stereotypes in identifying sports teams or mascots.

Rainforest or savanna   These are the terms to use in lieu of jungle, suggests the Association of Educational Publishers—hence Tarzan of the Rainforest.

Rainmaker   The person in a law firm or financial organization with a reputation for being an important figure with extensive contacts and name recognition, whose job it is to generate growth for the business by attracting significant clients and to put together the mega deals that ensure high profits for the company.

Ramp up   A term popular in the cyberworld for the introduction of a new process or product.

Rapid oxidation   Nuclear plant talk for a fire.

Ratchet up   To escalate or increase pressure, using the metaphor of a ratchet wrench's action.

Rationing by hassle   A health insurer's practice of first denying responsibility for paying for medical services. If the consumer persists, the appeals procedure is so complicated and time consuming you often throw up your hands and fail to pursue rightful claims.

Razor blade theory   The manufacturer's scheme of pricing products such as computer printers and razors at low prices because the real profits pour in when the consumer purchases the pricey blades and ink cartridges.

Razzies   These are prizes awarded annually in Los Angeles as the verso of the Academy Awards. Golden Raspberry Award voters choose the worst picture, the worst actor and actress, the worst screenplay and the worst director. There is even a trophy for the worst supporting performance.

Receive our free brochure   An introduction to a company's product that allows that company to pester you forever.

Recovered components   The language of NASA to describe the bodies of astronauts found after an explosion of a space ship.

Reckless Sex   A term tossed about by lawyers and legal scholars for penetration, sans condom, in a first-time sexual encounter. Their hope is to criminalize the act to cut down on the spread of AIDS and help would-be victims of date rape.

Red herring   The preliminary prospectus for proposed company financing. The name comes from the prominent warning notice on the cover paper, sometimes even printed in red ink, alerting potential investors to the risks inherent in investing their money in the offering.

Red state   A term for those states that went for George W. Bush in the 2004 Presidential election. We survivors of generations schooled on the Red Menace and Red China are expected to change our former ideological color coding to this new media driven tinting. The term for those states that went for John Kerry in the election is blue states, and purple states are those states whose voters split.

Redlining   Once a term used by the military for clearing traffic off a communications line awaiting an important message or pulling a plane off flight status; it also refers to an illegal tactic used by lending institutions whereby they discriminate against declining neighborhoods and their typically minority populations by refusing to extend mortgages or loans.

Reduced product demand   Another way of saying poor sales.

Reduction activities   The process of firing workers. If you have been part of a process "to eliminate redundancies in human resources," you just got fired.

Re-engineered   A former position (yours) has been moved from its former place in the company structure. In fact, the position has been shifted to the dumpster outside. In short, you're fired.

Reflect   A verb that was once employed at graduation ceremonies and by aged statesmen in their final moments. It is used by present-day politicians to mean that they will be doing additional analysis on that issue because not one pressure group has, as yet, won them over. If one has, they have no intention of announcing their position.

Reflection room   Students these days are no longer banished to a room for detention for misbehavior but to a reflection room.

Registered representative   The modern appellation for a stock broker.

Reinventing government   The concept underlying the special project headed by Vice President Gore in 1993 to streamline and reorganize government bureaucracy through an American version of "a great leap forward," in order to serve the nation more economically and efficiently. The consequence was that a record number of civil service jobs were eliminated as tasks were restructured, some positions were outsourced to private firms, office landscaping eliminated walls in favor of carrels, and more administrative layers of top level functionaries were created to superintend those efforts than in any other Administration.

Relationship manager   If you were hired at Chase Manhattan to sell accounts, you go by this moniker these days, rather than salesman.

Removes embarrassing stains   Of course, one wonders about a product that says nothing about non-embarrassing stains, and what those might be: coffee, catsup, grass, or that old stand-by, the bleach you have dribbled on your clothes while filling up the washer.

Representative   Besides the term for your elected member of the lower house of the US Congress, a present-day add-on to sales or travel to mean salesperson. Often the term replaces the old term, "man."

Reservation specialist   Another name for travel agent.

Resource development park   Your city dump.

Resources-control programs   Pentagon-talk for poisoning the vegetation or water supply of the opposition during military campaigns.

Restructuring   The corporate management tactic of shutting plants or dramatically cutting the work force to make the company appear to be more profitable for shareholders and prospective investors. Persons who are fired are, of course, "restructured."

Resume gap   The space that is left unfilled in the work history of those who have been out of the job market for some period in their adult lives that requires explanation and rationalizing for prospective employers. Those particularly effected and subject to scrutiny include housewives and mothers, individuals who have been incarcerated and those who have endured prolonged illnesses.

Revectoring   The term used by companies ostensibly to describe redirecting the course of business operations invariably results in a change in the corporate arrangements to achieve dramatic reductions in the size of the work force.

Revenue enhancement   A favorite phrase proffered by Presidents and the Congress to make the notion of any increased tax sound as if it might be a less painful means of adding to the federal treasury.

Revenue sharing   The deceptive practice by which mutual fund companies share with brokerage firms a portion of their management fees to induce them to sell their products to unsuspecting clients. Instead of offering objective advice the brokers push the sales more strongly for the funds that pay them best.

Reverse discrimination   The situation in which members of the majority feel themselves to be discriminated against during the process of providing balance for minorities who have historically been victims of discrimination. Such charges have been levied against company and government hiring practices and university admission policies where minority members—once discriminated against—are now reaping preferential treatment.

Revolving door   The pathway between government regulatory agencies, purchasing departments in the private sector, or the reverse, whereby officials move back and forth with their know-how and just as frequently their know-who.

Right-brained   What we used to call talented students, as opposed to those we called smart students who achieved high SAT scores and went off to great schools on scholarship. Studies show that arts and literature students show a tendency at right-hemispheric dominance and end up being supported by the disposable income of left-brained persons who majored in engineering, science, business and commerce.

Right-to-work laws   From this language you might conclude that this has something to do with the literal right to a job. Ironically you would be mistaken. There is no such thing as a right to work in any state. These laws actually restrict worker rights. Such laws outlaw "closed union shops" thereby promoting "open shops." An open shop is a company that employs workers without regard to whether they are members of a union. These laws ban workers, who by a majority vote may decide to form a union, and their employer from negotiating union security clauses. By such laws unions must represent all workers, both members and non-members, in contract negotiations and other workforce issues. A union security clause does not force workers to join a union but simply means they must pay a fair share for the economic benefits they receive because of union representation, such as health insurance, pensions and salaries that are on average better than those for non-union workers. A right to work law allows non-members to get all the benefits of union members and pay nothing while forcing unions and their members to cover the bill for those not willing to pay their share. The consequence is to weaken unions with insufficient resources to represent their members.

Rights   The Bill of Rights spells out the list of what the government cannot do to violate individual rights in protecting your life, liberty and pursuit of happiness. Legislation governing the civil rights of people with disabilities extends their rights to such things as medical services, employment, social security, physical and mental health, education and the enjoyment of our common cultural heritage.

Right-sizing   Downsizing would be a more precise way to announce reductions in the work force of a company.

RINOs   Acronym coined by the staunch conservative wing of the Republican Party for those Republican members of Congress, typified by Senator Arlen Spector of Pennsylvania, whom they view to be "Republican in name only." The label identifies those not zealous enough in their voting records by failing to march in lock step with the far right's well-known views, e.g., social values (have we no workhouses?), federal spending (cut) and abortion (don't).

Road map   When coming from the lips of Henry Kissinger it described a set of principles or guidelines to work toward—involving the anticipated actions of several countries, but often, as critics noted, was nothing more than political window-dressing, since his statements made a circuitous route around more substantial terms such as accord or agreement. The term continues to live on in Bush II press statements. In 2002, for example, before Secretary General Kofi Annan, Danish Foreign Minister Per Stig Moeller and Russian Foreign Minister Igor Ivanov, President Bush explained that a "road map is a way forward, ... it sets conditions... is a results-oriented document... it's a way to bring people together so that they share their responsibilities;" in short, what would have been called a plan if there had been more substance to it.

Roadblocks   In the youthful days of television, the term meant to broadcast the same ad at the same time on all three major networks. Now, the concept has bounced to the Internet, where the same banner ad simultaneously proclaims the wonders of a new product whether your portal is AOL, MSN or Yahoo. A 2003 Ford F-150 truck ad, for example, introduced in this manner, was seen by 50 million Web surfers, and is believed to have boosted sales by 6 percent during the first three months of the campaign.

Robo-litigation   The automatically generated legal threats sent to consumers suspected of stealing satellite services, music and movies. The process appears to have replaced the evaluation and judgment of an attorney with a computer program that simply spews forth form letters.

Rocketing   The term marketing experts use to describe the buying habits of a group who will purchase big ticket products like luxury trips and flashy cars while pinching their pennies in everyday shopping.

Role stereotyping   At least one school test publisher's guidelines warns its writers against showing Asian Americans as academics, African Americans as athletes, Caucasians as business people, or women as wives and mothers.

Room temperature IQ   Term used by supercilious software designers, applied to typical end users, and their expected lack of the ability to understand and use their elegant creations.

Rugged individualism   A term employed primarily by the right, for the view that anyone can achieve success if he or she works hard enough without government interference or support. Among the more racist or reactionary, the implication is that those who do not achieve are the shiftless welfare-addicted minorities.

Running the table   Drawn from billiards or pool to describe the player who wins by clearing the table of all the balls consecutively without missing a shot. In political jargon, it implies a victorious sweep.

Rustbelt   Those Midwest and Northeast industrial landscapes whose monumental steel and textile plants have long ago locked their gates, leaving behind, like ancient fallen pillars, rotting neighborhoods and shattered lives of those without the means to compete in today's economy.

S

Safe house   Once a secure haven for international spies, it is now, more commonly, a site providing sanctuary from domestic violence and sexual assault.

Safety net   The minimum level of funding to pay the costs of human services the government puts into place, ostensibly to salvage the unfortunate needy at the lowest level of society.

Safety users   Those who own cell phones only to make emergency calls to 911, since this is universally possible in the US without subscribing to a paid service. Many are senior citizens.

SAIEWDNBIFSWHTUTAAWTTTSTCOTFW   The abbreviation stands for the catchy phrase "Struggle Against Ideological Extremists Who Do Not Believe in Free Societies Who Happen to Use Terror as a Weapon to Try to Shake the Conscience of the Free World." President Bush II suggested replacing "the war on terror" term with those words during a meeting in August 2004 with a group of minority journalists. "We actually misnamed the war on terror," he said.

Sailor mongering   A 19th century maritime law meant to stop brothels from luring sailors to shore. Former Attorney General John Ashcroft's attorneys attempted to use this law for the first time in May 2004 in Miami's federal court to prosecute six Greenpeace activists who boarded a ship carrying 70 tons of mahogany near the port of Miami-Dade and unfurled a banner reading, "Stop illegal logging." US District Judge Adalberto Jordan issued a rare directed verdict finding Greenpeace not guilty before the case went to a jury because the prosecution's evidence did not prove that a crime had been committed.

Sanitary landfill   Your city dump.

Sanitize   The specious language used in the military and clandestine agencies for censoring. Also part of the ever-welcoming phrase, "sanitized for your convenience," found stretched across your toilet seat in lesser motels, implying the bowl has been cleaned since the last tenant used it.

Sales associate   The modestly paid clerk of yesteryear now has this more prestigious title but performs the work for about the same pay.

Satisficer   In a culture of affluence and super-abundance, the matter of choice can fuel anxieties for some in their selections of everything from which computer to buy to their next pair of shoes. "Maximizers" are obsessed with the need to own only the very best, often without regard to price differences. Satisficers, on the other hand, tend to accept what they deem to be good enough, limit their worry about the options they reject, reduce their expectations to reasonable levels and assume an attitude of gratitude for what they acquire. In his book, *The Paradox of Choice, Why More Is Less,* social theorist Barry Schwartz borrows from economics, psychological and market research thinking to put those questions into a balanced and reasoned perspective.

Saturday night special   Once a tabloid writer's term for a second-rate handgun, now used in the computer software industry to suggest an inelegant, cobbled-together solution to a product design, issued without review to meet an impossible deadline.

Save   Once used in conjunction, in reference to your soul. More recently, this cautionary term has turned its attention to your computer data and when last you secured it. For without attention, as we all fear, your data could end up, much like the clerical injunction regarding your soul, lost.

Scaffold learning   This has nothing to do with an about-to-be hung prisoner's newly acquired conscience, but is an educational term meaning the strategy of providing stepping stones provided by a teacher to advance a learner from task to task, helped by the knowledge gained in the process. If you ask a child if she sees three birds in your front yard, and two fly away, how many are left, that is scaffolding. Soon, the child can do the math without the support structure, and you move on from there.

Scenic route   A picturesque alternative to freeway travel, whereby you forgo the most direct route to a destination to travel the countryside behind a tractor-drawn cultivating machine. You'll see long-abandoned small towns, their main street a mass of for-rent signs and thrift shops. The sole gas station closed at dusk and your only lodging choice is a musty tourist court whose rooms reek of tobacco smoke.

Scheduled generation   Named for the kids whose overzealous parents rocket them from one meaningful activity to the next: swimming lessons, piano practice, after-school soccer, little league, birthday parties, scouts, and Sunday school, leaving moms, dads and kids road weary and the van ready for trade in.

Schlock   Another colorful import from Yiddish to convey any type of cheap or trashy merchandise.

Schmatte trade   This is how insiders characterize the garment industry —borrowing the more colorful Yiddish word for rags.

Schmoozer   Drawn from the Yiddish verb for informal talking or chatter, this has been transformed into a description for someone who draws upon beguiling charm in speaking with all manner of people, using personal charisma to persuade the listener to consummate business or political deals.

Secluded   Real estate term meaning the house has a non-functioning septic tank, is impossible to get public transportation to work from and features a dirt road that washes out at every storm.

Second strike capacity   The retaliatory might of a nation theoretically to have the power to reciprocate with nuclear weapons to a surprise enemy attack, no matter how great the devastation of the assault. The objective is to deter any such first strike.

Security moms   Concerned mothers identified during the period leading up to the Presidential election of 2004 as making electoral choices based on the candidate's position on national security.

Security violation   In the State Department and in overseas embassies, offices are inspected each evening for classified documents that should have been locked up. If the security staff in the State Department or Marine guards overseas discover a classified item on your desk or if your file cabinet or safe is unlocked, you receive a "security violation," a form of reprimand. If you receive several such reprimands within a given period, disciplinary measures are taken. However, given the need to finish an urgently needed report, or because of the nature of report and memoir writing among diplomats, secret materials are routinely removed from "secure" areas by top officials. If officials get caught, in those "inadvertent" removals, it makes the news. Thus, we read in 2000 that former CIA director John Deutch had "top secret" memos on his home computer, that retired Ambassador Graham Martin, in 1978, was driving around in Virginia with a trunk full of classified documents related to his posting in Saigon, and that in 2004, Samuel "Sandy" Berger, President Clinton's national security adviser, removed secret documents from the National Archives without permission and "failed to give them back." Possibly, hands are slapped when the biggies violate the rules, but if so, gently.

Seismic occurrence   What lab-coated scientists call an earthquake.

Select   A real estate term meaning a house that is presentable. In groceries, foodstuffs that have not passed their expiration date.

Select grade   Grade-creep reached the Department of Agriculture in the 1980s, when your steak, purchased at what was formerly stamped in purple as good, referring to its fat content, was promoted to select.

Selected out   A State Department and US military term for their officers' reaching the authorized span of years for a certain grade, after which they must retire or be fired. The timidity of those evaluating their underlings makes this a useful tool; the organization does not have to prove you are not good at your work, only that others at your rank were seen to have aptitudes and training that made them better at performing at a higher grade.

Selected response   This is how multiple choice test questions are referred to in contemporary educational jargon.

Self-contained   Used by entertainment industry agents to describe musicians who can perform independently since they work with CD players or sequencers to produce music (musicians call them Karaoke machines) and therefore do not need other instrumentalists to accompany them.

Self defense   The nation's assumed right to launch, without warning, a preemptive attack on another, when the Administration perceives the nation is threatened in a way that is contrary to its interests.

Self esteem   A term most often used with persons lacking in what once was viewed as self-confidence, the verso of which is another outdated term, self-satisfied.

Self-made millionaire   Someone said to have worked his way up from humble beginnings—with no money, no connections, sometimes little formal education—to live out the life of a Horatio Alger hero by dint of dedication, hard work, talent, a propensity for risk taking and natural entrepreneurial skills to found and build a business empire.

Self-regulation   A child psychology term indicating a maturation level leading to responsible behavior; a business term meaning the foxes are guarding the hen house.

Sensitive but unclassified (SBU)   This has nothing to do with a biological specimen but has replaced the term, "Official Use Only" in the State Department, and means the material should be protected from public disclosure as outlined in the Privacy Act. Also sometimes, if the document were picked up by the media, it could embarrass the government office involved.

Sentencing guidelines   The term refers to the US justice system's legal framework for sentencing convicted federal defendants. The guidelines have grown to an unfathomable mix of commentary, amendments, examples, policy statements and rules that, are, in fact, much more than guidelines. First, the judge must impose at least 25 percent of the maximum sentence, with little room for lessening the sentence due to the age of the defendant, his or her mental, emotional or physical condition, personal obligations, personal history of military or public service or other circumstances. Second, if a judge were to not follow these guidelines in sentencing, the sentence would likely face reversal in appellate courts. The American Bar Association recently recommended an end to mandatory sentencing guidelines, a view that was seconded by Supreme Court Justice Anthony M. Kennedy, in June of 2004.

Set the predicate   An inside-the-beltway term meaning to establish the groundwork for a political or military action, or to nudge public opinion towards a hoped-for view.

Service rate   This term softens the blow that you are paying interest on something.

Service level adjustment   A National Park Service evasion for cutting the number of days a park is open, ranger tours and exhibits, due to the Bush II Administration's budget cuts.

Servicing the target   Department of Defense-speak for killing and maiming enemy troops.

Seventh floor   Oblique State Department term for their bosses, since the Secretary of State and those known as Under Secretaries work on that floor of the State Department building. A high correlation between occupational status and office placement is the rule of thumb in overseas embassies as well, albeit, the CIA floor is often, for communication reasons, located now on the top floor.

Sex industry worker   A term elevating the status of a prostitute to the more neutral concept of a workaday business person.

Sexist   The calculated denigration by a member of one sex (usually male) of someone of the opposite sex, in speech, the workplace, government, politics, academia or social situations. The practice, however and wherever it is perceived—sometimes accurately, sometimes less so—is righteously lambasted in public expressions of every type, by all who carry on the ceaseless struggle to achieve equal treatment for human beings without regard to gender. There are doubtless innumerable times and situations where people clearly betray their bias against women by their derogatory verbal expressions. At the other extreme is the close monitoring of unacceptable, disrespectful language replacing it with politically correct but amusing substitutes—retroactive coverage instead of a grandfather clause, city leaders for city fathers, informed agreement for gentlemen's agreement, and first-year student for freshman.

Shared values   This was a short-lived 2002 public relations campaign by the US State Department's Public Diplomacy wing to combat anti-American sentiment in Arab countries. The campaign used visiting speakers and a $15 million TV advertising campaign, featuring Arab Amerians talking about life in the US. The ads were discontinued after a month. The project was an initiative of former advertising executive turned Undersecretary of State for public diplomacy Charlotte Beers, whose Madison Avenue approach to selling America to the world was as nuanced as the Shopping Channel. She arrived at State in October 2001 and resigned for unspecified health reasons in March 2003.

Shark repellents   The tactics used to discourage corporate raiders from takeover attempts by selling off key assets, employing golden parachutes and staggering the terms of board members making it harder to gain control of the board of directors.

Shelf life   If a can is bulging ominously at your local grocery, it has passed its useful shelf life. The term has been expanded to refer to the public's interest-to-disinterest span for fad diets, political scandals, a pop star's marriage, and books offering economic panaceas by former cabinet members.

Shock and awe   An overwhelming, fast and punishing military first strike used by journalists to describe the first stages of the invasion of Iraq; also known as blitzkrieg, practiced by the Nazis in Europe in WWII.

Shockumentary   A television show or video using clips of filmed accidents, grisly autopsy footage, cannibalism, and assorted violent acts of man against man allowing you to "relive the horror" but without the stigma of either watching professional wrestling or enduring something that is too educational.

Shoppertainment   TV programs long on commercial shopping pitches, with entertainment being reserved to wondering how the glamourous hosts fell to such depths in their acting career.

Shtick   Used to describe a characteristic trait or unusually personal way of doing something, currently used to identify the style of stand-up comedians. It is a Yiddish term, first used to describe the antics of Borscht Belt entertainers.

Significant   A verbal lubricant, an intensifier, applied like butter by spin artists to such terms as advance, book, discovery or event.

Significant other   Sociologist G.H. Mead introduced this term in the 1920s. It has come to mean the person with whom one shares a life—either with or without the benefit of matrimony.

Silent majority   The idea persists that there is a group of citizens who constitute the majority of the voting population, who seldom express their views in public forums but demonstrate their feelings only in the voting booths. The problem for politicians is identifying who they are, where they are and then, how to influence them since their actual values are anyone's guess.

Silk stocking liberal   The label from the right for those of the liberal persuasion, who themselves enjoy all the finest things in life while perennially bemoaning the plight of those at the bottom of the heap.

Simplistic   A term used to denigrate your opponent's sound-bite solution.

Single payer system   A health care plan used by most of the industrialized nations including Canada. It is characterized by the government functioning as the financial provider for medical services. All those who work are taxed to pay for it and everyone who requires care receives it at little or no added cost. Doctors and hospitals are paid by the government, thus avoiding the costs of paperwork necessary when private insurance companies are involved. The term to describe this by the right is socialized medicine.

Situ-tainment   An advertisement for a commercial product that is integrated in theme with the program being broadcast. The March 2, 2004, *Wall Street Journal* suggests that a courtroom drama could have a "car insurance commercial to look, sound, and feel just like the show it is interrupting."

Skills mix adjustment   The person doing the mixing is the personnel director and if you have been participating in such an activity, you just got fired.

Skip the middle man   Goods being offered have, it is assumed, mysteriously appeared at this location, since the store is not where the item was made.

Skyscraper ad   Marketing term for an online Web ad, or a banner that is much taller than the typical vertical banner advertisement.

Small houses   At least one textbook publisher wants you to use this term when discussing African dwellings once known as huts, on the grounds of ethnocentricity.

Smart   Not IQ in today's jargon, but an implanted circuit board charged with tasks as disparate as keeping track of your credit card withdrawals, and in a military weapon, making it much more selective in where it explodes and thus who it kills.

Smart border   The designation for the federal program instituted to sharpen surveillance methods to apprehend terrorists entering into the US from Canada as part of the new security tightening measures of the post 9/11 period.

Smokestack America   A characterization of those industrial companies, such as steel plants and automobile factories, that lost ground to imported products and modern technology, their once robust economic power but a memory.

Soccer moms   Suburban mothers relentlessly transporting their uniform-clad offspring to matches and other organized activities who maintain a dedication to the task only found in an earlier time among pony express riders.

Social networking   Web sites are the venues that attract people who are desperate for attachment. This system seamlessly connects those desirous of contacts for business, dating and friendly (or over-friendly) chats.

Social safety net   The ever-shrinking network of government agencies that care for others: health care assistance to those with disabilities; welfare assistance for dependent children; and unemployment insurance and other social programs that the needy can fall back upon during times of adversity.

Socialized medicine   One of the terms to denigrate and attack any system under which complete medical aid would be provided to every citizen through public funding. Other such appellations include nationalized medicine, state medicine and national medical insurance. The strongest opposition consists of political conservatives, doctors' professional societies and the insurance industry, all of whom decry such a socialistic idea even while the US remains the only significant industrialized country without some type of universal health care for its people.

Soft on crime   Label applied by conservative political candidates who prey on citizens' fears of crime, by targeting more liberal candidates for such positions as opposition to the death penalty or not favoring longer and mandatory punishment for those convicted of crimes. These conservative candidates, however, display far less passion about coughing up the funds for constructing more prisons to house all those convicted and ignore any correlation between automatic weapons used in robberies and their insistence that such weapons are a requisite for squirrel-hunting Americans.

Soft on immigration   Another element of the conservative litany, this one directed against those who support and believe in more generous immigration quotas and rights for legal and illegal immigrants, for fear that unless the number of new arrivals is sharply restricted they will overtax the nation's resources.

Soft power   The ability of the country to achieve its aims by displaying the attractive features of the society like its culture, political ideals and reasoned politics, rather than by threatening other nations, behaving in a belligerent diplomatic style or by paying countries to align themselves with us. In ideal terms American prospects for achieving success against terrorism is unlikely to succeed without more effectively combining soft power with military prowess in forging a position of "smart power," according to Joseph S. Nye, Jr., author of *Soft Power, the Means to Success in World Politics.*

Softening up   During the second Iraq war, Pentagon press releases used this abstraction describing dug-in "elite Republican guard" units' deaths by concussion, shrapnel and burning phosphorus. A Department of Defense news release of May 19, 2004, uses the term "soften up" for the torture of Iraqi prisoners of war during interrogation.

Sole-source contract   Uncle Sam's contracting of needed goods and services can be restricted to a single source if the specifications for the needed item or service are so unique that they can only be effectively met by a single company. There are many unique products and services, for example, a specialized medical device, that would require a sole-source contract. But it has not escaped bureaucrats' attention that a sole source contract is easy to rig by adding unique specifications—bells and whistles that only one supplier can offer—and it has not escaped the attention of the media and the House Government Reform Committee that Halliburton Company, which was awarded a sole-source contract worth billions of dollars to support the war and reconstruction in Iraq, was the same company that Vice President Cheney used to direct. On March 15, 2005, the Los Angeles Times reported, "Pentagon auditors said Halliburton Corp. might have overcharged the US by more than $100 million on a contract to deliver fuel to Iraq in the early days of the war." On March 17, 2005, the Houston Chronicle reported, "an Illinois grand jury has accused a former Halliburton Co. worker and a Saudi colleague of scheming to overcharge the Pentagon for supplying fuel tankers for military operations in Kuwait." Representative Henry Waxman, Democrat, commenting on Halliburton contracts for the reconstruction of Iraq, noted that the Bush Administration may have had valid reasons for granting a contract without competition for emergency war work, but, "it is harder to understand ... what the rationale would be for a sole-source contract that has a multiyear duration and a multibillion dollar price tag."

Some assembly required   The brazen assertion on innumerable packages that cues even the least sophisticated purchaser to plan on spending a good part of the next weekend struggling to put the product together. The instructions all seem to be written by a cousin of the foreign factory owner who claims to know a little English.

Sonofusion   The method of building commercial fusion energy generators by emulating the reactions that cause the sun to shine, producing fusion which would create cheap and virtually limitless electrical power. Current experimentation is under way under the auspices of the Pentagon's Defense Advanced Research Projects Agency, with first reports raising the possibility that this may prove feasible. At least one small company, Impulse Devices in California, is already making and selling equipment that some see as the next important step, which ultimately might free the world from its dependency on oil and coal.

Sorry 'bout that   A term meaning, basically, forget-about-it.

Sound bite   A concise statement lasting 20 seconds or so of mostly single syllable words, which is used to convey simple, brief news items for television, on the theory, proven time and again in recent elections, that the viewing public has neither the attention span nor the intellect to cope with subordinate clauses or more complex vocabulary.

Sound science   A propagandistic phrase used by polluters, pesticide firms and George W. Bush in speeches and White House press releases. There is no scientific substance to the term, but it is used to support decisions based on Administration policy, rather than policy based on peer-reviewed scientific evidence. The term may have been invented by an advocacy association (now defunct), The Advancement of Sound Science Coalition (TASSC), whose industry-friendly findings included views on global warming, smoking and chemical pollution. "We've got some regulatory policy in place that makes sense," Bush lectured youth award winners on April 24, 2004, "but it says we're going to make decisions based upon sound science, not some environmental fad or what may sound good—that we're going to rely on the best of evidence before we decide."

Special event   A program, action or happening that involves public participation or competitive activities, orchestrated to attract publicity and media attention to those sponsoring an occasion for a cause they favor.

Special interests   All the groups who are seen by conservatives as demanding legislation and financial support to further their purposes, such as women's groups, the aged, the unemployed, students and environmentalists. Conversely, liberals define special interests as comprising such factions as trade associations and their lobbyists, the corporate elite, banking and financial institutions and others seen as currying favor from the Congress and the White House for the benefit of their well-heeled constituencies.

Special purchase   What an upscale store calls marked down or lower-cost goods.

Spend more time with my family   A face-saving explanation that continues to be the favored explanation of departing bureaucrats and business executives who were asked or forced to resign. Among the more recent users of this term are former CIA director George Tenet and Tina Brown of the failed magazine, *Talk*.

Spenny   An unfortunate addition to English used by mall crawlers, replacing the adjective expensive or the more modern pricey.

Spiffs   The word used by the marketing fraternity for gifts or cash inducements offered to retail store managers or sales personnel for promoting the sale of their products.

Spin control   Government and corporate communication wizards who manage information, thereby controlling the speech or comments by putting the material in the most favorable possible light for the public. The phrase is derived from tennis where players control the spin of the ball they hit.

Spinner   While once just a revolving fishing lure, the term now refers to a cyclist who apparently has not discovered the gear box, thus must constantly peddle rapidly; or in cyber talk, a slow-loading Web site, causing the little loading symbol to endlessly revolve.

Spinning out of control   Once a racing term, meaning that the driver has lost control of the car on the course, it now refers to the loss of orderly progression; a government that in a crisis spins out of control and no longer is following established processes.

Sports A business offering fame and fortune to professional athletes; a social binding for bar-room habitués; the last flourishing of baroque prose to journalists; and meaning to the lives of Red Sox fans.

Spyware The term used to describe software that appears on a computer unannounced and most often unauthorized, frequently as a result of the user having subscribed to a free service such as a file sharing network, or having agreed to a message in return for gaining access to a Web site. Spyware programs can range from being relatively harmless to distasteful and even illegal. They can feature pop-up ads, some for porn sites, and can slow your computer's speed because of the weight of those unwanted programs. The most dangerous spyware programs illicitly monitor Internet use, even capturing and recording your keystrokes for the purpose of stealing password entries.

Stabilizing the area A military term meaning people are still trying to kill you, but things are bound to improve at some point.

Stage phoning The practice of ostentatious individuals who make believe they are talking into a cell phone when they are just trying to get attention and impress others.

Stagflation The societal condition which perplexes economists when rising price levels coincide with relatively high unemployment numbers.

Standardized test An examination designed to determine the academic progress or achievement of students across a school district, state or the entire nation. Controversies arise over the use of such testing instruments when they form the basis for promotion or graduation. Many parents as well as educators decry the idea. They reason that "teaching to the test" denigrates or even eliminates other important curricular components.

Star wars The Ronald Reagan Administration's design for the Strategic Defense Initiative, which sought to create weapons to be deployed in outer space to repel the Soviet Union's intercontinental ballistic missiles. Those who opposed the program saw it as a costly federal boondoggle to enrich defense industry contractors. The program relied on flawed testing information and never proved workable. The name was lifted from the popular film with the same title.

Starter home   Real estate term for a tiny house the seller wants to unload on a young couple or single person who either does not have need for more space, or if they do, they are not about to get it.

Starving the beast   The epithet used by those who strive mightily to under-fund what they regard as costly and unnecessary government funding. They are particularly suspicious of research and development in scientific, technical, environmental, and health areas, no matter how promising the results and pervasive the benefits.

State of the art   Once a term referring to the culmination of a particular technology, it is now a Madison Avenue term meaning new model.

Statesman   A politician who has left office by reason or age or electoral defeat who continues to serve on commissions and boards that issues observations unheeded both at home and abroad.

Status quo   Those with money and power like to hold on to both. If life is a boat ride, they do not want anyone changing course: preferring their own firm hand on the rudder and sailing established routes. Liberals and those left of center continually ask, what if and point in new untried directions, while accusing conservatives of seeking to preserve existing conditions to safeguard their interest. Thus liberals, tempted by new directions and not tied to the established ways, are more disposed to advocate economic and social change, which conservatives see as threatening to them and all they hold dear.

Stay the course   Searching for an exit strategy from an untenable position, used frequently by politicians who lead us into quagmires, and generals explaining why American forces are still there.

Stealth inflation   This is that dire economic specter that results in higher prices from all manner of firms, from banks to phone companies to hotels to credit card companies, all of which manage to extract more money from you without actually raising their rates.

Among the imaginative devices used by the billing companies to jack up their prices—and usually overlooked on your monthly bill—are mysterious money-raising fees such as "regulatory assessments," "handling charges" and "restocking costs."

Sterile zone   A shoot-to-kill security parameter surrounding a high level meeting site, such as the G8 summit of world leaders. To protect the conferees from the thousands who routinely turn up to protest globalization, armed police, concrete blast barriers, high metal fences and patrolling military aircraft are employed. It is not unusual for as many as 25,000 police and military personnel to be deployed to counter efforts to disrupt the meeting or to counter terrorist threats. Such security measures rule out meetings in urban areas.

Still finding (his/her) way   A polite way for parents to summarize a son's or daughter's unsuccessful search for gainful, satisfying employment other than some short-lived jobs that help with the car payments.

Stonewall   To obstruct justice by revealing little or nothing to cover up the truth. The term came into modern use when Richard Nixon employed this verb in instructing his underlings to say nothing during the Watergate affair in the 1970s. The term probably derives from the behavior of Confederate General Thomas J. Jackson, who was nicknamed Stonewall, after forcefully holding the Union Army at bay in the first battle of Bull Run in 1861.

Stop-loss orders   In the past this term was best known as a device investors instructed their brokers to follow to sell stocks once they had declined in market price to a specific level, in order to insure against any further loss should the stock continue to drop. More recently it describes the military's stated policy that allows commanders to hold soldiers past the date they are due to leave the service if their unit is scheduled to be deployed or redeployed to the Middle East, to prevent a mass exodus of combat and other essential troops before a tour in the combat zone.

Street lit   Publishing jargon for popular pulp fiction.

Stress positions   CIA and US military term for an extraordinary interrogation technique in which prisoners are handcuffed and shackled in standing or awkward squatting positions for a long time, disallowing rest or sleep and causing muscles to cramp and the shackles to cut into their bodies. This technique was approved for use by the White House for interrogating al Qaeda prisoners until the Abu Ghraib prison scandal in Iraq focused media attention on the practice. As of June 2004, the practice was suspended, pending "review" by the Justice Department.

Strict constructionists   Those members of the Supreme Court who judge a case by looking at it from the vantage point of a narrow and literal interpretation of the US Constitution without concerning themselves with the changes in our society and its technological evolution since that document was written in the 18th century. Or, if they are "broad constructionists," they extrapolate from the language in the Constitution what they judge to be the intent of the drafters, and they interpret sections of the document to address, in our complex society, our current needs and standards of social behavior. The Court noted for its broad construction interpretation was under Chief Justice Earl Warren, whose members, through its many decisions changed much of American life, such as Brown v. the Board of Education, reapportionment, the ban on school-sponsored prayer, and the Gideon and Miranda rulings. Strict constructionists, who attempt at times to modify decisions of previous "broad constructionist" courts, believe it is the job of a Supreme Court justice to interpret the law, not make law. *See also Activist judges*

Stud book   Long used in reference to the published pedigrees of dogs, horses and an ancient slang term for the Social Register, it is still used in the diplomatic community in reference to the Biographic Register. Until 1975, this was an open-sale annual government publication providing concise biographic information on personnel of the Department of State and many other federal agencies in the field of foreign affairs, listing colleges attended, former jobs in and out of government and postings abroad. Cynics claim that it has two obvious uses: diplomats writing holiday greeting cards use it to find forgotten names of spouses and the KGB and sister organizations employ it to identify CIA personnel working in embassies under clumsily disguised designations. For, as was disclosed 30 years ago in books and magazines, if the stud book listed someone as "foreign service officer reserve" (FSR) rather than a Foreign Service Officer (FSO) appellation, it was an *indication* the person could really be working for the CIA. This system of finding CIA employees by leafing though this easily obtained publication resulted in (1) the murder of CIA officers, (2) hazardous lives for embassy secretaries, agricultural attaches, AID workers, physicians, printing plant staff and others working abroad who were in fact, FSRs, (3) State's sensible decision to no longer publish an unclassified version of the directory, and (4) dropping the use of the designation FSR.

Student   This is the term political correctness demands we use; the major educational publishers have banned the term *coed* from their books.

Stuff happens   This variant of a motorcycle thug's "shit happens" was employed by Secretary of Defense Donald Rumsfeld in April 2003 to shrug off the looting and violent civil disorder that took place after the invasion of Iraq, with absolutely no acknowledgement of the human and cultural horrors of those events.

Sub-prime lending   The practice of providing a mortgage for someone considered below the conventional acceptable level, yet deemed creditworthy enough to buy or refinance a home in spite of a blemished credit history. The practice flourishes because it is often part of predatory practices by some lending institutions, which load borrowers with steep fees and unnecessary add-ons. Not uncommonly, these types of loans are elements of a deceptive marketing strategy that does not fully reveal the full cost of the loan, and are often concentrated in low-income communities where residents have limited alternative options. The result often is gouging the borrower and leads, in many instances, to foreclosure.

Subsidy   The extra compensation paid to corporations to counteract price instability or market weakness, and as an inducement to deliver goods or services, seen to be in the national or security interest of the nation. Uncle Sam pays corporations to deliver goods or services that would otherwise not be able to continue at the present level—due to market weakness or price instability. However, your corporation has to convince Uncle that continuing production is in the national or security interest of the nation. This is not very difficult. Stephen Moore, Director of Fiscal Policy Studies at the Cato Institute, testified to the House Budget Committee that, "all but a small handful of America's most profitable corporations have participated in the hunt for federal or state government subsidies. Most of these companies are double-, triple-, and quadruple-dipping. In 1996 General Electric Company won 15 grants for $20.1 million. Rockwell International received 39 grants for $25.4 million. Westinghouse Electric Corporation received 14 grants for $26.1 million. Yet each of these companies had profits of at least half a billion dollars that year."

Substance abuse Vulgarly known as drug addiction or drunkenness.

Substandard housing A slum by any other name.

Sudden reputation death syndrome A malady recently afflicting corporate titans who are enmeshed in shocking public revelations of questionable financial machinations, as in the case of Dennis Koslowski or Bernie Ebbers.

Suffragist A host of American textbook publishers are now using this politically correct term for those courageous women who fought to get the right to vote, women once known as suffragettes.

Suggested retail price A common fiction proposed by the manufacturer, and frequently printed on the package or price tag, typically bearing little relation to the actual selling price of products from t-shirts to cars.

Suicide bombing The term used to cover the sacrifice of one's life to kill and mangle your political or religious opponents. In military operations, such as WWII, young kamakaze pilots were trained to use their plane as a last-ditch weapon against military targets, taking their own life when the plane exploded on target. An alternative is the random killing and maiming of men, women and children as a method of attempting policy change or simply an act of reprisal, as in the 9/11 attacks. Strapping bombs to a volunteer for such "sacrificial operations" has become increasingly common in Israel and Iraq.

The Quran (verse 2:51) prohibits suicide, but not sacrifice in a just struggle, thus the use of the sacrificial operations term.

Suits   The negative stereotyping of white business men attired in dark suits, who demonstrate complete lack of sensitivity toward all but the corporate bottom line.

Super patriots   That unique class comprised of extreme bigots who combine fiercely nationalistic passions with a severe distaste for minorities.

Superpower   A nation with real or imagined power over other countries, because its citizens and its leadership believe they can profoundly influence other states and the balance of international authority. A superpower's strength is seen to derive from its unrivaled military and economic strengths.

Supply side economics   The idea is that tax cuts cause economic growth. Well, not just anyone's tax cuts (not yours for example) but cuts for big business. With higher profits due to those lower taxes, the supply-siders claim, companies will invest their savings in industrial growth. Your next leap of faith is that once those corporations start spending, production increases, jobs grow and then new workers start paying taxes, making up for the tax cuts to industry. With greater production, the price of goods decreases and your purchasing power goes up. With all those bargain prices, you rush off to buy more stuff, and thus, Uncle also collects more taxes from working stiffs. The popular press called it "trickle down economics." How about the loss of tax revenues? Not important. The economy would outgrow them. The architect of this theory was Arthur Laffer, then an obscure economist, who advised Ronald Reagan during his first Presidential race. Reagan's rival candidate was George Bush, who termed the theory "voodoo economics." Reagan won the election, and charged his brilliant budget director, David Stockman, to make it work. Thus, tax cuts were enacted in 1981, and rather than the predicted 5 percent growth in 1982, the economy suffered its worst year since World War II. In 1986 Stockman confessed in his book, *The Triumph of Politics,* that the 1981 tax cut "was a Trojan Horse to bring down the top (tax) rate for the wealthy."

Support group   What we used to call close friends and caring relatives.

Surgical safari   Travelers who journey to South Africa for plastic surgery and then follow it up by going on safari while they are healing. Known also as a scalpel safari.

Surgical strike   An air raid with the intent of obliterating only the military target. In reality, such precision is rare and there are usually unforeseen consequences: maybe the target is smashed, maybe it almost is smashed, but when the high-tech ordnance explodes, it wreaks havoc on innocent victims.

Surplussed   If you learn you are surplussed, that means you are no longer needed in a company, and you've been fired.

Sustained deep undervoltage   When the lights go out in hundreds of thousands of homes during a widespread system breakdown; a term coined by the electrical power companies.

Sustained silent reading   Children who once read in school now practice you-know-what, or SSR for the initiated. Kids refer to it as, "sit down, shut up and read."

Sweeping the board   To dominate in a situation, derived from basketball, when a player controls the rebounds off the backboard.

Sweetener   Offered on restaurant tables in lieu of sugar packets, and to decision-makers in government contracts in lieu of honest competition.

Synergy   The mystical and frequently mythical force which is assumed to work its wonders when two corporations merge, resulting in unimaginably rosy benefits in efficiency, economy and profitability for the succeeding company; to say nothing of the dizzying level of rewards doled out to the corporate managers as well as the investment firms who make it all happen.

T

T-group   A seldom heard term these days, but familiar during the 1960s and 1970s. The concept was popularized by Kurt Lewin, a psychologist recognized for his help in the management of critical government agencies during World War II. The idea was to form a group in an organization to collect information about how people feel about that organization, their unit and the surrounding unit's organization to identify sources of inefficiencies and alternatives. It fell out of fashion in the 1970s, however, when it appeared that such group observations had minimal impact on the larger systems of the organization, and employees began rolling their eyes at still another corny exercise in the process of "developing trust" among the participants with a few staffers dominating the process with their long-winded observations, and the "facilitator's" attempts to elicit "what you honestly feel." One delightful outcome of this process, however, was to drive a spike through the heart of the lecture method in training employees.

Take charge of your life   What once was known as getting organized or looking out for yourself.

Take out   This may still mean dating in teen talk, but for the military and clandestine services it is still another way of saying to kill or bomb a person or target.

Talking heads   The description for the high profile members of Congress, top government officials and assorted well-known pundits from the media and think tanks, who use the TV broadcast airwaves to convince the viewing audience of the virtue of their point of view on any and every issue under discussion.

Tall organizations   Classic illustrations are the government and the military in which there are countless layers of hierarchy from top to bottom. In contrast, the flat organization, epitomized by the Catholic Church, maintains a global complex with just five levels from the Pope to the priest in the parish.

Tandem work crews   The old fashioned appellation was chain gangs.

Tanker accident   In deference to the sensibilities of the oil shipping industry this is an oil spill in open water.

Taste tribes   Members of special interest groups drawn together by common cultural concerns who come together via the Web.

Tax base broadening   Reforms proposed by at least a dozen Senators would change the tax base from income to consumption, claiming this would simplify the tax system, make Uncle Sam less intrusive and possibly make it easier to save. Critics of these proposals claim that tax problems stem from difficulties in measuring the tax base. Others worry their mortgage interest exemptions would disappear.

Tax loopholes   The legal way to avoid or evade taxes that are legislated by the Congress with the advice and consent of their constituent beneficiaries who are the recipients of the largesse.

Tax sharing   The notion that because of steep federal taxation, it is difficult for state and local governments to exact their rightful toll, necessary to carry out their programs. The thinking then, is that Uncle Sam should kick back to the local jurisdictions some of their receipts, and that such funds could be used as local jurisdictions see fit and not as the US government requires. Naturally, not many in the Congress are very sanguine about the concept.

Tech-nouveau   The growing genre of commercial designers making use of current technology to produce shapes and forms found in nature such as flower petals. This process is sometimes called biomorphism or neo-organicism.

Technical violation   Illegal activities that are adjudged by their per-petrators as well as the reviewing authorities to be only a matter of minor misconduct and therefore subject to wrist-slapping penalties that seldom result in formal prosecution.

Teflon   A non-stick coating used to describe those political person-ages with the formidable quality of having no bad things stick to them to sully their reputations. President Ronald Reagan epitomized this trait when only those around him were charged with crimes dur-ing the Iran-Contra fiasco.

Termination with extreme prejudice   This is a term that describes killing a suspected spy without a trial that originated during the Vietnam War.

Theory x and theory y   Once popular management terms, identify-ing two views of the workforce. The terms were introduced in the 1950s by psychologist and college president Douglas McGregor, who supposedly developed his theories based on industrial studies, but likely spotted theory x examples on his faculty and only wished he had a few theory ys. Theory x holds your employees hate work and will go to great lengths to avoid it. Thus, management's job is to crack the whip to get any production from those lazy slobs, who lack ambi-tion, avoid responsibility, want security and prefer being ordered around. Theory y holds that in the right circumstances, work is a source of satisfaction, that committed staffers are self-directed and are emotionally rewarded for meeting their work goals, are creative in their efforts, and that the potential of the average worker is far greater than is realized.

Think tank   A simplified term for a complex organization, usually post-WWII, where a group of analysts from disparate fields address problems from their various fields and from their collective assess-ment. One of the earliest was the Rand (research and development) Corporation, made famous when its defector, Daniel Ellsberg, released a collection of studies on the Vietnam War, "The Pentagon Papers," which drove a coffin nail in the support for that war. Such organizations act as a bridge between the social sciences, science, technology and policymaking, with government and political action organizations being their largest customers, addressing issues as disparate as trade policy, world peace, military tactics and welfare options. Their sponsors and endowments ask not only that they produce solutions but, for those not doing classified research, publicize them, and today there is a full spectrum of such organizations, many with a political point of view, whose publications and spokespersons invariably reflect that political point of view.

Thinker   This was an epithet hurled at Al Gore by George W. Bush during the 2000 Presidential campaign, implying, apparently, an issue-focused, curious, wonkish quality, and not the kind of person the electorate is looking for.

Thinking the unthinkable   Actually addressing a dreaded outcome or unanticipated result, used as a reference for atomic war or if the opposition party wins the election.

This is just a test   First heard on your radio during the Cold War, in which the radio then emitted a low whistle or just plain silence. In the event of a nuclear holocaust, you might be too occupied or vaporized to listen.

Thousand points of light   Bush I used this term in New Orleans in 1988 in accepting the nomination for President. The phrase was the summation of a catalog of organizations including a bible study group, Hadassah and Disabled American Veterans, to illustrate his point of "a nation of communities...varied, voluntary and unique" that "spread like stars." Since this was a political stump speech, he implied that if everyone in those varied groups voted for him it would lead to a "kinder, gentler nation."

360-degree feedback   The latest wrinkle in performance evaluation techniques in which personnel are reviewed not only by just their bosses, but by colleagues, those they supervise and even clients.

Ticker shock   The malady affecting all those who watched their investments sink lower and lower when the stock market bubble burst at the turn of the century.

Timepiece   What New Yorker ads call a watch.

Tipping point   The means by which trends in behavior are based upon the accumulation of many small events until they snowball and become accepted as social norms. The phenomenon was first advanced by Malcolm Gladwell, a New Yorker writer in his 2000 volume, *The Tipping Point.*

To buy into   A term meaning that someone has suspended disbelief and will, in fact, support the promulgated position.

To dialogue   While often it means in educational jargon 'to discuss,' it has been absorbed, as well, by sensitivity trainers to imply valid give-and-take communication, rather than a run-of-the-mill, garden-variety conversation.

To impact   Media term meaning to emotionally affect a large number of people, or an exciting news story, good or bad, or an important event that meets the time slot criteria for the news media. Important topics that do not appear suddenly, such as the trade deficit or Burmese or Tibetan independence, do not have impact appeal and tend to be ignored.

To morph   A computer graphics term referring to the changing of form, of transforming a picture from one image to another, often with startling results, and of course, derives from metamorphosis. A software program changes one picture or object to another by offering a string of transitional link pictures between the starting and ending pictures, using an animation program. Hollywood and videogames both make extensive use of the process, but software is now available to use the process in home movie videos and multimedia projects.

To process   To reflect.

Tombstone   A public announcement in a newspaper of a stock or bond offering. The designation is based on the black border around the printed matter.

Topless dancer   Not an escapee from a Washington Irving story, but rather a female performer *with* a head attached but *without* cover from her belly button up to her sequined lashes.

Totally awesome   A positive response in teen talk, meaning high praise.

Tourable   To characterize an author with the push, persona and profile to be suitable, in the publisher's view, for promoting the book on television and radio talk shows and at bookstore events.

Trade barriers   Characteristics of the country's economy based upon political decisions to restrict international trade, in order to strengthen the nation's own economy or selected industries within the country. A common barrier is a tariff on imports that enhances the profit-making potential of domestic companies, which are in competition with the imports from abroad. Sometimes such restraints can be voluntary if foreign concerns can be convinced to limit their sales in order to win political favor. Naturally, world and regional trade groups like the World Trade Organization, the World Bank and the International Monetary Fund seek to limit all government-imposed barriers in the interest of an open and competitive trading environment.

Trade promotion authority   In the past, Congress gave authorization to the President to negotiate trade deals without subsequent Congressional modification, called fast track authority. But the term seemed to imply a too-rapid rubber-stamping of the pacts; thus the new label.

Trade safeguards   The term which Administration officials prefer to straightforward language, like tariffs on imports—the word safeguard implying the government is warding off unfair competition from less costly goods from abroad.

Traditional healers   Those practicing medicine who operate without state or medical society license and care for the ill using various animal and vegetable potions, the reading of bones and divination. European travelers of yesteryear used the offensive term "witch doctors" for these practitioners.

Traditional values   That favorite slogan of political rhetoric which means different things to different people, but for countless Americans the term usually embraces conventional marriage and family, personal morality, integrity, a strong work ethic and individual freedom. In Britain and Canada, the list might also be extended to include honesty, tolerance, courtesy, honor, peace, order and equality. Groups which typically associate themselves with traditional values invariably are supporters of a role for government in fostering the promotion of those values.

Transfer pricing   An international shell game whereby major US multinational corporations shift profits to countries with lower tax rates, bilking Uncle Sam. In 2002, Pamela Olson, then Assistant Secretary of the Treasury for Tax Policy, told a Congressional committee that "the inappropriate income shifting that results can significantly erode the US tax base." A May 18, 2004, Washington Post article notes that in fiscal year 2003 corporate taxes represented just 7.4 percent of federal revenue, down from 32 percent in 1952." The same article quotes financier Warren Buffet's remark, "if class warfare is being waged in America, my class is clearly winning."

Transport rule   This is the term which was used by Michael Leavitt, the Environmental Protection Agency's Administrator under Bush II. Under Bush II's Administration, the EPA rescinded a regulation that required power companies to install pollution-control equipment when upgrades of their plants would increase pollutants. In its place was the Leavitt-proposed transport rule concept, whereby prevailing winds from west to east simply blow away the polluted air more cheaply than expensive filtration equipment. Misinformation, stated the EPA's inspector general, Nikki Tinsley in 2004, who is not a political appointee of Bush II. She suggests that EPA had misinformed Congress about the potential impact of revoking this key rule governing pollution from power plants, and that there was no basis for the new rule in science or law.

Transportation counselor   The counsel here takes the form of persuasion in selling new or used cars to prospective customers.

Travel counselor   A travel agent.

Travelers   The role of a publisher's sales representative, who visits colleges to sell instructors on a company's textbook line, and to elicit interest from professors who may wish to consider writing a textbook.

Trial lawyer   Wordsmiths who supply Republicans with terms designed to prejudice the listener suggested using "personal injury lawyer" rather than the less emotion charged "trial lawyer" when

T

referring to the 2004 Democratic Vice Presidential candidate John Edwards.

Trickle down economics   The promise that a rising tide lifts all boats, suggesting that helping large corporations and the wealthy through tax benefits and subsidies will provide help as well for you and me. The theory was debunked after it failed during the Reagan Administration, but that has not prevented its resurfacing during the George W. Bush Presidency when the lion's share of the deficit-building tax reductions have rewarded the rich, with the rest of us looking at the sky and wondering when the trickle will start.

Trickle down nuclearism   A description for those have-not nations with no nuclear arsenal that wish to imitate the efforts of those that do have the capacity to deploy such lethal weaponry. The appeal of owning one's own bomb extends to small non-governmental, terrorist, religious or political groups, who have obtained nuclear weaponry by purchase or theft in order to further their own sinister objectives.

Turkey farm   Government civil service regulations make dismissal of an employee for other than criminal offenses an overwhelming task. This point is not lost on Uncle Sam's bosses, who find it simpler to relegate these doofuses to areas outside of the central thrust of the organization. Thus the less critical a division is to a department's mission, the more likely it is to be filled with a collection of incompetents and political appointees, busy drafting memos to one another. A variant in the foreign service are entire countries filled with American representatives fitting this category, the thinking being we don't care what goes on at that backwater as long as it doesn't get back to Washington.

Tweens   A Madison Avenue term for America's 8- to 12-year-olds who, more often than not, have a television and radio in their room, and maybe even a video-game player. What we used to call kids are now a targeted market worth over $15 billion a year in sales, and better yet, are still on the bottom rung of that golden ladder of consumerism.

Twonky   In software design jargon, a needless appurtenance placed there at the behest of the marketing department. The term was first used in a classic 1942 science fiction story, "The Twonky," by Lewis Padgett.

Type T The marketing community's characterization of the sort of person willing to assume risks in making consumer choices.

Ugly American A widely used pejorative designation for arrogant, tasteless and insensitive Americans who travel abroad and view everything they experience through the prism of American standards of living, while remaining incurious and ignorant about foreign customs and cultures. The term is derived from the title of a book by Eugene Burdick and William Lederer, which depicted American officials in a mythical Asian country.

Un-American The derogatory labeling still heard on occasion from conservatives and ultranationalists to assault the point of view of those with whom they disagree or who hold values inimical to their own.

Uncertainty factor A term used by the Environmental Protection Agency identifying the components of those informed guesstimates that affect your life. EPA specifically identifies some of these uncertainties: variation in sensitivity to a substance from person to person, extrapolating to humans what happened to a test animal, figuring out what damage has been done during an exposure to something harmful or when the study covers less than a full life span and use of LOAEL data (see definition) rather than NOAEL (see definition) data.

Uncompromising A term often used as a modifier in military briefings, as in uncompromising standards, uncompromising stance or uncompromising devotion to duty. A sort of Styrofoam packing to help the noun along.

Underclass   In a culture that prides itself on the absence of class structure, this phrase characterizes the poor, the homeless and the downtrodden—often made up disproportionately of blacks and Hispanics—who live below the subsistence level with only the remotest prospect of ever improving their economic position.

Underdeveloped   To characterize countries that have little wealth or other resources to redistribute to their impoverished populations, nor sufficient financial resources to offer welfare or even minimal social, economic, educational and health services to its people. Many place the blame for this plight on long years of colonialism followed by despotic and corrupt rulers.

Underprivileged   Once upon a time there were poor people. Then they became deprived, disadvantaged and finally underprivileged. But it still means those at the bottom level of the economic scale without the means or the governmental initiatives for bettering their condition.

Undertakers   Businesses that buy distressed merchandise for resale at rock bottom prices.

Undocumented immigrants   Illegal foreign workers on whom countless employers rely for minimum wage labor. Formerly known as wetbacks, from crossing the Rio Grande, the current slur is illegal alien.

Unreal issue   The National Evaluations Systems ask that you use this term in place of what they regard as sexist: straw-man.

Unselected rollback to idle   When a prop plane suddenly loses power in an engine.

United States Chamber of Commerce   This business organization, officially named the Chamber of Commerce of the United States of America, has absolutely no connection with the government even though some may be misled by the popularly used appellation. It is not against the law to use 'United States' as part of the name of a non-government organization, e.g., US Steel Corporation.

Universal coverage   The phrase for health care insurance for every-one—a concept that is still a dream in the US and a fact in most other developed western nations.

Up the ying yang   A slightly politer way of saying stuffed up one's ass.

Upscale   Anything seen as characteristic of what is owned, sought after or admired by those who aspire to the upper rung of the eco-nomic ladder.

Urban whitefish   New York sanitation workers' term for used condoms.

US policy   An educational test developer's guidelines ask you to use this term rather than *American policy*, which could be taken as geo-graphical chauvinism.

User fees   Another form of collecting taxes from those who avail themselves of government services, such as National Park Service admission charges.

User friendly   An advertising term meaning that you can actually operate the equipment without reading the instruction manual. However, the spin-agent who wrote that advertising copy was in fact thinking of a rocket scientist's use of the equipment. Further, since most user manuals are not understandable, the term has lost most of its meaning.

Utilize   A Latinate term beloved of bureaucrats and military briefers, meaning to use or employ.

Vacation specialist   A travel agent.

Vehicle-mounted active denial system (VMADS)   What you do is strap what looks like a large satellite dish on the top of your "mobile platform"—read Humvee—and push a button that fires bursts of electromagnetic energy at people up to a quarter mile away. It is a sort of mobile toaster, heating the skin of your victims to 130 degrees, causing intense pain and directing them away from the weapon, or, in Pentagonese, "to influence motivational behavior" with a "long range, anti-personnel, non-lethal force." It's called "active denial" because it actively herds people. It is not known if this people zapper could be adopted for use in the cattle industry or for crowd control at Liverpool soccer matches.

Velvet revolution   Refers primarily to the few weeks in November 1989 when a popular upheaval ended Communist rule in Czechoslovakia, led by thousands of protesters demonstrating in the streets of Prague. The term is used as well to describe other mainly bloodless transfers of power in some—but by no means all—newly independent states in Eastern Europe. The transfer of Hong Kong back into the People's Republic of China and the Gorbachev-led changes in Russia have also been referred to by the same term.

Vice-versa virtuecrat   The cohort of those who crusade against moral relativism and in support of strict adherence to standards of right and wrong, as they believe standards of right and wrong to be.

Vietnam syndrome   Reluctance on the part of Americans to send troops to fight abroad for unclear objectives that grew out of the tragedy of the 1954-1973 Vietnam War. Bush I, celebrating his victory over Saddam Hussein in Iraq in the 1991 Gulf War, declared "the Vietnam Syndrome is buried forever in the sands of the Arabian peninsula." But the Vietnam Syndrome appears to have dampened a national consensus in supporting the Bush II War in Iraq, questioning the rationale, the "axis of evil" concept, now-you-see-them-now-you-don't weapons of mass destruction and the absence of a viable exit strategy.

Viral marketing   A Web marketing concept in which the customer passes along a marketing message to another customer. This is the email equivalent to word-of-mouth marketing.

Vision thing   A sweeping expression invented by President George H. Bush referring to all those positive goals one finds in State of the Union messages. A sort of shorthand for aspirations like world peace, freedom, democracy, full employment... panaceas one's speechwriters scribble, but which are difficult to bring into being. The American historian Henry Adams said that the President "resembles the commander of a ship at sea. He must have a helm to grasp, a course to steer, a port to seek. While the Constitution awards the President the helm, creative Presidents must possess and communicate the direction in which they propose to take the country."

Vital interests   The concerns that are commonly construed to be of broad overriding significance to the country such as its safety, vitality and survival. Important elements include the security of its people and the protection of its infrastructure from attack. Commitments that are consensually agreed upon as enduring elements include the principle of democracy, human rights, individual liberty and the rule of law. The more cynical might add the safeguarding of our untrammeled access to petroleum.

VNR (Video news release)   In early 2004, local television stations in Oklahoma, Louisiana and other states aired a short television video in which reporter Karen Ryan "helps sort through the details" on the 2003 Medicare bill, saying, "there have been a lot of questions about how the law will help older Americans and people with disabilities." Critics noted that there was no indication in the video that Karen Ryan was hired to play the role of a reporter and was reading a script prepared by the US Department of Health and Human Services. HHS had sent the tape to local television stations across the country. A spokesperson for HHS defended this electronic boilerplating, whereby the watcher sees a manufactured news story without attribution, believing it to be a legitimate local news story.

Vocal minority Those groups that express their displeasure with government programs or policies through public expression or demonstration, thereby provoking other citizens to wonder about the questions. Also a method of officially dismissing views other than your own by implying that the majority agrees with your views, but just has not taken the trouble to say so.

Vocational relocation If your boss uses this term while holding a pink slip, you know you are on your way out the door—permanently.

Voice theft The illicit use of someone else's recorded or synthesized voice to gain access to a voice-activated security system.

Voices of Civil Rights An initiative to build the world's largest archive of first-hand accounts of the civil rights struggle in the US by recording accounts of those who participated in the fight to end segregation and promote racial equality in the 1950s and 1960s. Sponsors of this program include AARP, and the Leadership Conference on Civil Rights. A group called the Freedom Writers is collecting the interviews and will be turning their files over to the Library of Congress.

VOIP With this prospective new protocol, Voice-over-Internet (VOIP), consumers can make telephone calls over the Internet. In the maelstrom of competitive zeal and swift technological adaptations in the telecommunications industry, VOIP may be the next wave, with a number of companies already at work to bring it into widespread popular use in the coming months. If that comes to pass it should hold the potential of ultimately rendering obsolete much of the $125 billion traditional telephone company industry, and they will have to find some new method of billing for their services.

Voluntary termination In the nicest possible way, you are being told you are fired.

Wake-up call   A favorite term of politicians and advocacy groups who point to an incident and extrapolate the anticipated results if there is not an immediate change of policy.

Wardrobe malfunction   The bizarre characterization of singer Janet Jackson's sudden breast-baring during a Super Bowl halftime entertainment sequence. Janet's "bust-see TV" not only infuriated thousands, but prompted Congressional "nipplegate" hearings and an FCC crackdown.

War of liberation   The term for the Bush II invasion of Iraq.

War on drugs   The expression conjures the notion of a kind of tactical military campaign to rid society of the scourge of narcotics by stopping the traffic in illicit drugs at their source, during their transport and at the point of sale and use. But after many years this pseudo-war rages on with few visible signs that victory is anywhere in sight. Similarly, various Administrations have employed the vapid term "war on poverty" and the more recent "war on terrorism."

Warts and all   A term, first coined by Oliver Cromwell, to describe at least a modicum of negative comment in a book, article, or other media coverage.

Water feature   A term TV gardening shows use for those unnaturally natural waterfalls, ponds and fountains which teams of landscape gardeners stuff into suburban backyards. Hopefully, the term will not migrate over to the travel channel, so that we hear talk of the water features of Piazza Navone.

We have some history   A term implying a past relationship, often of a sexual nature.

Weapons of mass destruction (WMD)   Born most likely in Vienna's UN Offices of Arms Control, the term means big, terrible weapons of all sorts that are not necessarily under the monopolistic control of a traditional military force and have the capacity to kill spectacularly large numbers of people. These can be chemical, biological, nuclear or radiological in makeup. Historians of spin will note that the original purpose of Bush II's invasion of Iraq was to seize those threatening WMDs. None were found, the information on their presence being "badly sourced." *(See entry)* Now we are told the ongoing war is inculcating democracy in the region and there is nary a word about those pesky WMDs.

Web hosting   A company that provides online services for a Web site, the connectivity, storage and services related to maintaining a site. A variety of backup services are available from the thousands of Web hosting companies to help with e-commerce: toll free numbers, "shopping carts," and secure servers.

Web log *see* **Blog**

Wedge issue   A term for a political or social issue that attracts strong support or opposition and can be used to insert internal dissent in a political party. When the Bush II Administration introduced a proposed Constitutional amendment banning single sex marriage, clearly a cause that would not garner enough support for passage, the intent was to make Democratic politicians take a stand on the issue, causing dissent within the Democratic Party.

Weekend pill   The popular term applied to the recently introduced male drug to combat impotency—Cialis. While Viagra's effect lasts only a few hours, this newer one is said to work for up to 36 hours.

Welfare   From the perspective of the far right this is seen as the government's system of rewarding the indolent, with the American taxpayer footing the bill.

Welfare cheats   A widely believed myth that a major portion of those receiving public assistance are little more than chiselers fully able to support themselves if they wanted to but preferring to feed at the government trough, and further, that mothers on welfare bear even more children simply to ensure that their payments will not be decreased.

Welfare queen Derogatory spin term used by the reactionary media to characterize unemployed black women.

Western values The seemingly inoffensive phrase causes critical listeners to wince when they hear politicians attribute such common beliefs to most Americans while never defining precisely what in the world they are talking about.

Whatever Today's weary response to a non sequitur or to an unusual, strange or shocking remark you just can't garner the energy to discuss. In more formal times, the response to such a statement was, is that so or really?

What's in, what's out A roster of our culture's current passions, fads and favorites, including places, products, foods, fashions, music, TV shows, and celebrities; the hot, temperate and soon-to-be-forgotten. "In," according to the cognoscenti, are the people, places and things at the peak of popularity; "out," of course, points to that which was formerly admired and sought after, but now, a short while later, is embarrassingly, hopelessly passé.

Wheels-up party A State Department term for the joyful embassy celebration that follows the departure from the local airport of Air Force One (or Two) with its contents of Presidents, Vice Presidents, and assorted functionaries, still intact, but gone. The revelers have for weeks toiled in preparation, negotiated who goes through what door first, staged photo-ops, translated remarks for the press, marked standing spots for the President with duct tape, led shopping trips to the local market for the spouses, and finally packed and stowed the carpets, copper pots and other souvenirs on the plane.

Where are you coming from? A contemporary term questioning the rationality of a statement.

Where I'm coming from In simpler times, the phrase was "in my view" or "in my opinion."

Whiners and complainers   The term used in the 1980s by Senator Alan Simpson (R, Wyoming) for those Vietnam veterans who were alleging that their exposure to Agent Orange, a herbicide spray used during the war, had resulted in various kinds of cancer, skin disorders and other health problems. The link between Agent Orange and service-connected disabilities was confirmed in the 1990s.

White knight   Language to characterize a financial magnate or other firm arriving on the scene at the crucial hour to rescue a company and its management from a hostile takeover offering from a predator. The term derived from *Through the Looking Glass* by Lewis Carroll in which Alice is saved from the dreaded red knight by a white knight.

Wi-fi   The service more formally termed wireless fidelity, which is growing in national popularity as a means of gaining Internet access without a telephone line. Many new laptops have wi-fi cards built in, with coffee bars and other commercial venues providing reception, called hot-spots, for laptop-laden loiterers.

Wigger   A pejorative term for a white person who tries to emulate black culture, black fashion and speaks a kind of embarrassing ersatz hip hop.

Wiki   Software first created in 1995 and available on www.wiki.org, allowing you to create and edit Web page content. Useful for non-technical users who value content over form. It allows any number of contributors to work on a site, facilitating collaborative efforts.

Will we be tested on this?   The ego-bruising term used by students when asking an instructor—who has just presented a remarkable summary of materials gleaned from years of graduate studies—if the materials are, in fact, important enough to be remembered and possibly even studied after the class.

Wise-use movement   The term, while connoting a conservationist approach to environmental issues, is a loosely affiliated anti-environmental coalition, often funded by timber, mining and chemical companies, coveting use of public lands for extractive industries' use. Among the movement's claims are that the hole in the ozone layer doesn't exist, the chemicals dumped into the sky and water are harmless and that regulations protecting sensitive areas are violations of Fifth Amendment property rights, thus unconstitutional government "takings." The Bush II Administration's Secretary of the Interior, Gale Norton, was formerly employed by the Mountain States Legal Foundation, which reportedly provided free legal defense to wise-use groups.

With it   A term of approbation for those whose actions, dress and lifestyle are culturally in tandem with those making the evaluation.

Work through   What we used to term to endure.

Workforce adjustment   If you read this in your pay envelope, guess what, you're fired.

Working poor   The plight of countless millions of Americans, with heavy concentrations of African Americans and white single mothers among them, many of whom work full time but still earn too little and live at the poverty level.

Workplace diversity   The code word for broadening the base of employees who staff an organization to ensure the inclusion of blacks, Hispanics and females. A more apt and understandable description of workplace diversity would spell out what it really means by specifying the features of inclusion such as race, sex, sexual orientation and any other activity incorporated in the organization's plans.

World class   Used to describe pricey top-of-the-line options in travel, as well as a meaningless adjective used to exaggerate the importance of anything from pumpkin seeds to coaching techniques.

Would you like fries with that?   The phrase that launched a nation of fatsos.

Wuss   A weakling or ineffectual person.

You can be the proud owner This Madison Avenue staple fails to mention you will be the proud owner, as well, of monthly payments.

You guys How you are referred to—no matter how old or laden with degrees, decorations or honors—by restaurant employees, unless you are willing to pay for four-star service, in which case they use the simpler and less familiar you, that has worked so well for the past century or so. Sir and madam in address, is, of course, obsolete unless an employee is asking you to depart because you are causing a disturbance.

You may already be a winner This plaintive claim, featured in Web site banners and junk mail, is the marketers' desperate attempt to get you, through greed, to slow down and actually look at their offerings, rather than listening to your rational self saying "you may already be a loser."

Your call is important to us A canned corporate response to telephone queries eliciting a fingernail-on-chalkboard response from callers. Your prisoner-of-the-corporation status is further abused by unwelcome sales pitches, elevator music, and imbecilic repetitions of earlier messages. The prelude to the finale is a staggering memory test of numbers to push. Invariably, the one you want is listed almost as an afterthought, leading, with luck, to a genuine human being. Maybe your call is important to us, but not so important as our bottom line.

Your demographics are poor A term that strikes terror into magazine, newspaper or television executives. It means that you have failed to attract the core marketing target of persons age 18 to 36, the favored deep-pocketed set. Common wisdom has it that to attract this group, you need to thread onto the shish kebab of your media's offerings another mindless report on Margaritaville or J Lo's boyfriends. It need not be so, however. The fastest growing media outlet is National Public Radio, whose broad range of offerings attracts disparate groups with a delightful blend of well-developed topics.

Youthful figure This is politically correct; zapped by at least one textbook publisher is the term *boyish figure*.

Z

Zs Hip hop talk for sleep.

Zapped Military parlance for killing an enemy and hip-hop talk for exhausted.

Zen generation The description of the members of the beat generation of the early 1960s who were drawn to Eastern spirituality, particularly to Zen Buddhism, without receiving any formal instruction in the precepts. This in turn led to imprecise and fuzzy-minded notions about the true path of enlightenment, reflected in their writing, especially the works of Jack Kerouac. But the name stuck.

Zero tolerance The expression for policies that provide for the toughest police actions possible with no latitude in the strict administration of laws commonly used against drug sale and use, sexual predators and repeat offenders, even when such actions threaten civil liberties.

Zero-based budgeting (ZBB) A management technique that attempts, contrary to funding based on past budgets, to start with nothing (zero), then prioritizing what you want to do and attaching funding levels to each of those activities. President Jimmy Carter brought such a program with him to the federal budget from his days as governor of Georgia. To properly develop such a budget requires a huge investment in staff time at all levels, and then detailed review by knowledgeable experts. Since such experts were few and far between, the budgets looked suspiciously close to budgeting decisions based on previous funding levels. However, the process was useful in painlessly ridding departments of outdated Congressional mandates, things bureaucrats had long wanted to zap in any case, such as "book reviewing" staffers in the US Information Agency left over from the McCarthy era. Budget writers found they could justify their organization's requests by gerrymandering needed babies with institutional bathwater. Like most management techniques, if the institutional commitment was there to make it work, it did; otherwise, it was simply another management fad.

Zone of proximal development (ZPD)   Children gradually learn to do certain tasks on their own, such as opening the refrigerator. Educators claim this comes from following an adult's example, rather than say, an inherited ice cream-seeking gene. There are many things a child cannot do without help or guidance from an adult, such as riding a bicycle or wearing sensible clothes, and this area of need is called by educators the ZPD.

Zhuzhing   A word popular with the young hip culture, since it was coined on the TV program *Queer Eye for the Straight Guy*, for adjusting one's appearance by fixing such personal effects as one's hair or clothing.

Zig-zags   Hip hop reference to rolling paper, seldom used for tobacco products.

Zinger   A short caustic remark or retort, often viewed as funny by all who hear it except the recipient. Often employed on Las Vegas stages by persons billed as comedians.

Zipper problem   A not overly oblique term for President Clinton's sex scandal.

Zippies   The term applied in India to young men and women in their late teens to mid 20s, powerfully motivated to making and spending money. This group's employment often involves software programming and lesser skills out-sourced by American corporations.

Index of Terms

INDEX OF TERMS

BUSINESS TERMS (Continued)

INDEX OF TERMS

BUSINESS TERMS (Continued)

Lulu
Machers
Magalog
Management consultant
Management guru
Managing the blood supply
Manufacturing czar
Market timing
Marketroid
Matrix organization
Mature
McProfiling
Meetling
Meme
Merit system
Military industrial complex
Military procurement
Misery index
Mobility pool
Mompreneurs
MOP's
Moral hazard
Mousetrapping
Natural flavor
Natural order
Natural rate of unemployment
Negative economic growth
Negative employment growth
Negative employee retention
Negotiable
Neoconomy
Never needs ironing
New economy
Non-multicolor capability
Non-performing credits
On hold
On sale
On task
One per customer
One size fits all
Organization chart

Organoleptic analysis
Outplacement consultant
Outside the box
Paper or plastic?
Permission marketing
Persistency specialist
Peter Principle
Phishing
Phone ladies
Phood
PODS
Poison pill
Portfolio administrator
Post bubble anxiety disorder
Post crash realism
Post trauma job changer
Power alley
Power lunch
Preassembled furniture
Pre-owned
Presenteeism
Preventive sanctions
Price enhancement
Price points
Price supports
Product placement
Public broadcasting
Quaint
Rainmaker
Ramp up
Rapid oxidation
Razor blade theory
Receive our free brochure
Red herring
Redlining
Reduced product demand
Reduction activities
Re-engineered
Registered representative
Relationship manager
Removes embarrassing stains

INDEX OF TERMS

Representative
Reservation specialist
Restructuring
Resume gap
Revectoring
Revenue sharing
Rocketing
Revolving door
Reverse discrimination
Right to work laws
Right-sizing
Roadblocks
Robo-litigation
Sales associate
Satisficer
Schlock
Schmatte trade
Schmoozer
Secluded
Select
Select grade
Self-made millionaire
Self-regulation
Service rate
Sex industry worker
Shark repellents
Shoppertainment
Skill's mix adjustment
Skip the middle man
Skyscraper ad
Smart
Social networking
Sole-source contract
Some assembly required
Sonofusion
Special purchase
Spiffs
Spyware
Stagflation
Starter home
State of the art

Stealth inflation
Stop-loss orders
Sub-prime lending
Sudden reputation death
    syndrome
Suggested retail price
Suits
Supply side economics
Surplussed
Sustained deep undervoltage
Sweeping the board
Sweetener
Synergy
T-group
Tall organizations
Tanker accident
Tax loopholes
Technical violations
360 degree feedback
Theory x and theory y
Ticker shock
Timepiece
Trade barriers
Trade promotion authority
Trade safeguards
Transfer pricing
Transportation counselor
Travel counselor
Travelers
Trickle down economics
Tombstone
Turkey farm
Tweens
Twonky
Type T
Undertakers
Undocumented immigrants
United States Chamber of
    Commerce
User friendly
Vacation specialist

INDEX OF TERMS

BUSINESS TERMS (Continued)

CULTURE

CULTURE (Continued)

INDEX OF TERMS

CULTURE (Continued)

God's will
Gorelet
Graylisting
Great man theory
Greedy geezers
GU
Guilt free vacationing
Hair disadvantaged
Handcrafted
Hard line
Hardcore
Harvest
Have a good one
Have sex
Having a relationship
He doesn't get it
Headcount reduction
Health care
Helicopter parents
Heteroflexible
Heterosexist
High maintenance person
Histrionic Personality Disorder
Hockey dad
Holistic
Home
Home protection weapon
Hook-ups
Housekeeper
Human race
I feel your pain
In touch with your feelings
Inappropriate words
Indefinite idling
Infielder
Inner city
Intellectual
Intellectually stunted
Intelligent design
Interface
Interfacing electronically

Isn't that special
Issues
Jack-booted government thugs
Jefferson muzzles
Juvenile delinquent
Joe six-pack
Kitsch
The L word
Lad lit
Latchkey child
Law and order
Lay a guilt trip on
Leader
Law and order
Least best
Lesbo drama
Like so five minutes ago
Lipstick indicator
Low maintenance
Ludology
Magalog
Mainstream media
Maintenance person
Making a difference
Manufactured home
McMansions
Medicine of desires
Meet-up
Mess
Metrodox
Metrosexual
Micetronauts
Middle America
Midlife crisis
Mobile home community
Mobility challenged
Mobility pool
Model
Moderator
Mom lit
Mompreneurs

INDEX OF TERMS

CULTURE (Continued)

Mongo
Monoculturism
Mouse potato
Movieokie
Multicultural guidelines
Multiculturalism
NASCAR dad
Natural flavor
Natural order
Need
Needs work
Negative economic growth
Negative employment growth
Negative employee retention
Negatively privileged
Neo-con
Networking
New age
Next gens
Nicotini
NIMBY
No brainer
No problem
Non-believer
Nonmaritial birth
Not really
Not quite ready for prime time
Occupational stereotyping
Older persons
On task
One nation under god
Optimist
Overconnectedness
PACs
Painting a house
Parade of horribles
Partial birth abortion
Pearl tea
Person who can't hear or speak
Person who has arthritis
Person who is mobility impaired

Person who is non-disabled
People of the United States
People who are blind
Perp-walk
Pessimist
Pest control technician
Peter Principle
Physical attribute of abilities
    stereotyping
Pioneer
Plain brown wrapper
Plant superintendent
PODS
Poor
Pop
Porno-chic
Positive discrimination
Post-modern churches
Power walking
Pre-feminist
Pre-owned
Prenup
Pro- choice
Pro-life
Public waste reception area
Quality time
Quick and dirty
Racist
Rainforest
Ratchet up
Reckless sex
Representative
Reverse discrimination
Rights
Role stereotyping
Room temperature IQ
Rugged individualism
Rustbelt
Safe house
Safety users
Saturday night special

INDEX OF TERMS

CULTURE (Continued)

INDEX OF TERMS

CULTURE (Continued)

COMPUTERS AND THE INTERNET

EDUCATION

EDUCATION (Continued)

INDEX OF TERMS

208

INDEX OF TERMS

GOVERNMENT AND POLITICS (Continued)

Axis of evil
Backdoor draft
Background briefing
Backward country
Badly sourced
Bailout
Bay of Tonkin episode
Baseless
Beltway
Benign neglect
Big government
Biometric measures
Bipartisan
Bleeding heart
Blood in the water
Blow-back
Blue dog democrat
Blue ribbon panel
Boat people
Bork
Breeder document
Bundlers
Cabinet
Calculated risk
Camouflage candidates
Campaign consultant
Capital punishment as deterrent
Carnivore
Cash-flow
Character issue
Chicken hawk
Chief Justice of the Supreme Court
Civil commitment
Civil rights
Clarify
Class warfare
Classified information
Clean up the historical record
Clear skies initiative
Climate leaders
Coalition forces in Iraq

Coded messages
Collective punishment
Commitment
Common good
Compassionate conservative
Competitive bidding
Conceivably
Confederacy of the mind
Confidential memorandum
Conservation
Contract with America
Controlled communication
Controlled economy
Controversial
Core competencies
Corporate reform
Corporate welfare
Cost shifting
Covert operation
Credibility gap
Crime in the streets
Crowd management team
Cultural wars
Culture of life
Culture of poverty
Currency adjustment
CYA
Cyberspace activist
Cynical
Czar
Data mining
Data Quality Act
Death tax
Death with dignity
Debrief
Deep ecology
Deep six
Defense Department
Defense spending
Deficit
Delayering

INDEX OF TERMS

INDEX OF TERMS

GOVERNMENT AND POLITICS (Continued)

I hear you
Idea whose time has come
Ideologue
Illegal entrants
Immediate
Impact authentication devices
In God we trust
In one way or another
Inappropriate words
Incompetent
Independent counsel
Insourcing
Intercommunal warfare
Interrogation
Irrefutable evidence
Jack-booted government thugs
Jefferson muzzles
Junk science
Just war
Juvenile delinquent
Kickback
Kinder, gentler conservatism
Known knowns
The L word
Law and order
Lawfare
Leaving to pursue other options
Liberal
Liberal guilt
Likely
Limousine liberal
Lobbyist
Log cabin Republicans
Low-income
Loyal opposition
Lulu
Machers
Magical thinking
Making things perfectly clear
Malcontents
Managed news

Management consultant
Manufacturing czar
Massage
MATRIX (Multi-state anti-terrorism information exchange)
Mature
Meaningful dialogue
Member of Congress
MEMCON
Meetling
Merit system
Middle America
Middle Class Bill of Rights
Middle East road map
Millennium challenge account
Minimize
Mission accomplished
Mission creep
Misspeak
Mistakes were made
Moderate
Modern republican
MUF
My fellow Americans
Nannygate
NASCAR dad
Nation building
National intelligence estimate
National security strategy
Natural rate of unemployment
Neocon
Neoconomy
New federalism
New world order
Not for attribution
Nuclear option
OBE
OGA
Old Europe
One nation under God
Organization chart

INDEX OF TERMS

GOVERNMENT AND POLITICS (Continued)

INDEX OF TERMS

INDEX OF TERMS

GOVERNMENT AND POLITICS (Continued)

Western values
Wheels-up party
Whiners and complainers
Wise use movement

Working poor
Zero tolerance
Zero-based budgeting (ZBB)
Zipper problem

HEALTH

Abdominal protector
Accident
Afflicted
Attention deficit disorder
Auditorially challenged
Biosurgery
Birthing center
Book of life
Brownfields
Carb-avoids
Challenged
Choice
Chronologically challenged
Civil commitment
Clear skies initiative
Climate leaders
Code master
Community mobility
Conservation
Convalescent home
Culture of life
Dead shovel
Death with dignity
Deep ecology
Depopulation
Drug runs
Economy-class syndrome
Employer mandates
Erectile dysfunction
Eternity leave
Feng shui
Greenfields
Hair disadvantaged

Handicapism and
    handicapped
Hazardous waste
Health care facility
Hurry sickness
International medical
    graduate
LOAEL
Managed care
The Match
Medicine of desires
Meth orphans
Micetronaughts
Midlife crisis
Mild irregularity
Mobility challenged
Mortality rate
Motion discomfort
Negative patient care
    outcome
Nicotine Nazis
Nuclear accident
Nuclear event
Neutraceuticals
Partial birth abortion
People who are blind
Permanent global summer
    season
Person who can't hear or
    speak
Person who is mobility
    impaired
Person who is non-disabled

INDEX OF TERMS

HEALTH (Continued)

Person who has arthritis
Personal preservation flotation
    device
Phood
Plan B
Pollution rights
Poorly buffered precipitation
Post-bubble anxiety disorder
Power walking
Physically challenged
Pre-existing condition
Premium practice
Pro-life

Public waste reception area
Rationing by hassle
Sanitize
Seismic occurrence
Single payer system
Socialized medicine
Substance abuse
Surgical safari
Traditional healers
Uncertainty factor
Universal coverage
Weekend pill
Would you like fries with that?

MEDIA

Above the line
Action news
Acting presidential
Active consideration
Advertorial
Anchor person
Anniversary
Assault
Blood in the water
Bottom feeder
Brought to you by
Chattering classes
Commercial broadcasting
Confidential memorandum
Confrontainment
Controlled communication
Dittohead
Electronic surveillance
Embed
Encore TV broadcast
Enhanced radiation device
Evil biology
Faction
Flip flop

Graylisting
Greenwash
Hajis
Hexiform rotatable surface com-
    pression units
Hide and sleep weapons
High fratricide level
Hollywoodize
Human race
In depth study
Infomercials
Japander
Log rolling
Magalog
Mainstream media
Managed news
Media bias
Meme
Mindshare
Modernized translation
Mom lit
Not for attribution
Not quite ready for prime
    time

INDEX OF TERMS

MEDIA (Continued)

Off the record
Parade of horribles
Photo op
Public broadcasting
Pundit
Shelf life
Shoppertainment
Signifcant
Situ-tainment
Sound bite
Spin control

Street lit
Talking heads
To impact
Tombstone
Tourable
Tweens
VOIP
Wardrobe dysfunction
What's in, what's out
Your demographics are poor.
Zipper problem

MILITARY AFFAIRS AND INTELLIGENCE

Absorb
Action
Almost certainly
Anti-personnel weapon
Appropriate
Approved interrogation techniques
Asset
Asymmetric warfare
Background briefing
Bay of Tonkin episode
Biometric measures
Body bags
Burn rate
Calculated risk
Carnivore
Chokepoint
Civilian irregular defense soldier
Classified information
Clean bomb
Coalition forces in Iraq
Collateral damage
Collective punishment
Combat emplacement evacuator
Competitive bidding
Collateral damage
Conceivably
Converging forces

Core competencies
Covert operation
Dark biology
Debrief
Defense Department
Degraded
Depopulation
Detainees
Don't ask, don't tell
Dover factor
Electronic surveillance
Embed
Emergency exit light
Enemy combatants
Engage the enemy on all sides
Enhanced interrogation
    techniques
Enhanced radiation device
Embed
Ethnic cleansing
Evidence-free
Evil biology
Excessive volatility
Extraordinary rendition
Fear up harsh
First strike capability
Force flow

INDEX OF TERMS

MILITARY AFFAIRS AND INTELLIGENCE (Continued)

Friendly fire
God sponsored violence
Hajis
Hearts and minds
Hexiform rotatable surface com-
    pression units
Hide and sleep weapons
High fratricide levels
Human intelligence collectors
In one way or another
Incontinent ordnance
Intelligence specialist
Interrogation
Killing box
Known knowns
Lawfare
Liberate
Likely
Limited war
Malcontents
MATRIX (Multi-state anti-terrorism
    information exchange)
MEMCON
Military advisors
Militia
Mission creep
Mutual assured destruction
National intelligence estimate
National security strategy
Naval advanced logistic support
    site
Nuclear event
Nukespeak
OGA
Operation Desert Storm
Peace dividend
Peacekeepers
Physical pressure
Police action
Portal shields
Possibly

Pouch
Potentially disruptive re-entry
    system
Pre-dawn vertical insertion
Preemptive counterattack
Premature antifascist
Preventive detention
Resources control programs
Sanitize
Second strike capacity
Security violation
Selected out
Self defense
Servicing the target
Shock and awe
Smart
Softening up
Sole-source contract
Sonofusion
Stabilizing the area
Star wars
Stay the course
Sterile zone
Stop-loss orders
Stress positions
Stud book
Surgical strike
Take-out
Termination with extreme
    prejudice
Trickle down nuclearism
Uncompromising
Utilize
Vehicle-mounted active denial sys-
    tem(VMADS)
Vietnam syndrome
VOIP
War of liberation
Weapons of mass destruction
    (WMD)
Zapped

INDEX OF TERMS

SOCIAL BEHAVIOR

INDEX OF TERMS

SOCIAL BEHAVIOR (Continued)

SCIENCE AND TECHNOLOGY

INDEX OF TERMS